Jim Minor and his wife, Peggy, ... love their huge hearts for Jesus and for the poor. Through the years, we have had the privilege of witnessing their extraordinary generosity. They move in the power and the glory of God. In this book, with great humor, wit, and wisdom, Jim shares his many unique experiences as a pastor. Above all else, it is his passionate love for Jesus that shines through these pages. The affection that Jim and his church family have for our Savior enables them to feed the poor, heal the broken, and cherish the hurting. This book will energize you to recall the power of your first encounter with Jesus and fall in love with Him all over again.

—*Heidi Baker, Ph.D.*
Cofounder, Iris Global Ministries
Author, *Always Enough, Compelled by Love,*
and *Birthing the Miraculous*

This is the most helpful book for pastors that I have read in a long time. I can hardly recommend it enough! It is so well written, so fun, so practical, and so full of sensitivity, love, and joy in the Holy Spirit, that I believe it will help transform churches wherever it is read. No, churches shouldn't suck! They should be the very epitome of what Paul considered the only thing that counts: "*faith working through love*" (Galatians 5:6). Leading a church is no longer *work* for the pastor who is joined to Jesus and is one with Him. It is a family, full of believers overjoyed to bear fruit by actually doing the works of Jesus because they love Him so completely and are so energized by His Spirit. This book shows how a church can truly be *good news* to the poor, desperate, and lost, wherever they are to be found—whether inside the church, on the city streets, or throughout the world. Be encouraged and excited by this store of wisdom and experience written in complete humility for the sake of those hungry for the kingdom!

—*Dr. Rolland Baker*
Director and cofounder, Iris Global Ministries

I have had the honor of ministering at Pastor Minor's church and have witnessed for myself his contagious love for the broken. It is so refreshing to partner with a church that is so real and honest and that has such a heart to see the captive set free. I'm so excited for *Church Shouldn't Suck...the Life Out of You*—it won't disappoint! This book will refresh you, encourage you, make you laugh, and turn your heart toward loving God's people more.

—*Kim Walker-Smith*
Worship leader and recording artist
Director, Jesus Culture Music

While reading *Church Shouldn't Suck...the Life Out of You*, I smiled, laughed out loud, and nodded my head in agreement. I recommend this book for three reasons. First, I have been a member of The Harvest Church in Sarasota, Florida, for several years. I have seen the life lessons from this book at work each and every week. The lessons written here are not theory but proven truths that anyone can follow. Second, you will enjoy reading about how God taught Pastor Jim the definition of success in both life and ministry. Third, I have a friendship with every one of Jim's children, and they all are serving the Lord. When the children are walking with and working for Jesus, it confirms to me that the father knows what he is talking about. I know that the time you spend reading this book will be time well spent.

—*Dr. Roberts Liardon*
Author of the internationally best-selling *God's Generals* series

To know Pastor Jim Minor is to know a friend, a pastor, a teacher, and a builder of bridges within our community. In all of these roles during the many years I have known him, he has remained steadfastly committed to spreading the love of Christ in all that he does. His love of the gospel and his practical application of God's Word are evident not only in his preaching and teaching but also throughout this book. He has built, and continues to build, bridges in the community that connect people to Christ and to God's amazing Word! Our community is a better and richer place for everyone because of his contributions.

—*Carolyn J. Mason*
Sarasota County Commissioner
Former mayor, Sarasota, Florida

Church
SHOULDN'T
Suck

the *Life* out of you

JIM MINOR

WITH JOE STINSON

W

WHITAKER
HOUSE

Unless otherwise indicated, all Scripture quotations are taken from the *New King James Version*, © 1979, 1980, 1982, 1984 by Thomas Nelson, Inc. Used by permission. All rights reserved. Scripture quotations marked (KJV) are taken from the King James Version of the Holy Bible.

Some definitions of Hebrew words are taken from the electronic version of *Strong's Exhaustive Concordance of the Bible*, STRONG, (© 1980, 1986, and assigned to World Bible Publishers, Inc. Used by permission.).

CHURCH SHOULDN'T SUCK...THE LIFE OUT OF YOU

Harvest Tabernacle
209 N. Lime Ave.
Sarasota, FL 34237
www.harvesttab.com

ISBN: 978-1-62911-153-7
eBook ISBN: 978-1-62911-154-4
Printed in the United States of America
© 2014 by Jim Minor

Whitaker House
1030 Hunt Valley Circle
New Kensington, PA 15068
www.whitakerhouse.com

Library of Congress Cataloging-in-Publication Data

Minor, Jim, 1953–
  Church shouldn't suck the life out of you / by Jim Minor, with Joe Stinson.
    pages cm
  Summary: "Pastor Jim Minor describes how his street outreach organization changed from a vibrant, God-infused ministry into a conventional safe church that almost sucked all the passion for ministry right out of him—and how he got his passion back again"—Provided by publisher.
  ISBN 978-1-62911-153-7 (trade pbk. : alk. paper) — ISBN 978-1-62911-154-4 (ebook) 1. Minor, Jim, 1953- 2. Clergy—Florida—Sarasota—Biography. 3. Church. 4. Pastoral theology. I. Title.
  BR1725.M48A3 2014
  253—dc23
                          2014018635

1 2 3 4 5 6 7 8 9 10 11 **ᵾᴶ** 21 20 19 18 17 16 15 14

DEDICATION

To my grandma
Sophia Springer Minor (Honey)

I came to your home broken,
and your unconditional love mended me.

ACKNOWLEDGMENTS

Peggy—you have stood the test of time and remained faithful, silently paying the price over these last thirty-seven years that this book might be written. You are the glue that holds us all together, and there is no better wife and friend.

My children, Jim, Dan, Erin, Jonathan, and Matthew—you have made this vision your own with a passion to shift the current culture to a culture of the kingdom. Your love for Jesus and your desire to take the gospel to the nations have brought me great joy. No dad could be prouder.

My pastors, Dr. David and Lorraine Minor—you have shown me the Way. Your laid-down lives were my signpost and my guide.

Grandma Sophie Minor—you taught me how to love the poor and broken.

Dad—you always believed in me.

Mel Tari and Rolland and Heidi Baker—thank you for taking me deeper and lower still.

Pastor Beatrice LaMonte—thank you for giving a young, fiery evangelist a chance.

And to the Harvest family—thank you for all of your prayers and support over these last thirty years.

CONTENTS

FOREWORD

He was born in a very difficult and profoundly interesting period of human history. Yet it was God's appointed time. He could have been killed because of the pharaoh's decree, but he ended up being raised in his very palace. There is no doubt that God had a plan and a purpose for Moses. He was destined to be a leader who would set God's people free from the bondage they had endured for more than four hundred years. Moses tried to fulfill his calling by going about it the wrong way—by killing an Egyptian man. As a result, he spent the next forty years on a mountain in the *"backside of the desert"* (Exodus 3:1 KJV), learning vital lessons that would prepare him to fulfill his challenging and seemingly impossible mission. This experience could have sucked the life out of Moses, but instead, God chose to meet him in the wilderness.

His encounter with God in the burning bush set him on the right path to accomplish God's great and specific call for him in the best possible way. After challenging Pharaoh with demonstrations of the power of God, he led the people out of Egypt on their journey to the Promised Land. Pharaoh did not make it easy for him; his army pursued the Israelites all the way to the barrier of the Red Sea. It was there that God met Moses in a new way. Moses had heard God's orders and obeyed, but this time, God showed up in the form of a pillar of cloud and positioned Himself smack-dab between His people and the Egyptian enemy. (See Exodus 14:19–20.) For forty years, God's presence accompanied the Israelites with tremendous displays of His power and abundant provision, as Moses continued to fulfill the task that God had given him. He passed the baton to Joshua, allowing the next generation to bring the people all the way to their final destination. Moses was, first and foremost, a friend of God, which was the primary reason he succeeded in the assignment that he had received at the burning bush.

Like Moses, God has a call and purpose on Pastor Jim Minor's life. In *Church Shouldn't Suck…the Life Out of You*, Jim shows us the right way—and also the wrong way—to follow and fulfill God's plan for our lives. You will receive the vital life-lesson keys for your walk with Jesus that Pastor Jim has discovered in his own life and ministry. This will help you to avoid the same pitfalls along the way, and, most important, you will learn to unlock the secrets of a successful life and ministry.

It is my joy and honor to know Pastor Jim and Peggy Minor all these years, and for Joyce and me to be called their friends. I have personally witnessed what God has done through them, their children, and the church family at The Harvest Church in Sarasota, Florida. Through their generosity and selfless sacrifice, they have effected change and made a great difference in the lives of many. Their love for the poor and downtrodden, and the powerful ministry they have had over the last three decades, is a direct result of their intimate and unwavering love for Jesus and their passion for the lost. We have ministered together in many nations over the years, and their impact in the lives of the multitudes is genuine and undeniable.

I enthusiastically recommend this book, not only for pastors, but for all Christians who love Jesus and desire to have their lives count for eternity by making a difference in the lives of many in their generation!

—*Mel Tari*
Author, *Like a Mighty Wind*

INTRODUCTION

I once heard a farmer say that just because somebody can spell the word *manure* does not mean that he or she understands the practical application of it. Don't get me wrong; I am not comparing my dad's life story to a pile of manure, but I've spent a lifetime watching some people preach the gospel of Jesus with little understanding of how to apply it in a practical fashion. The entire gospel of my childhood was a life filled with the practical application of the love of Jesus to every confused, broken, and addicted castaway we crossed paths with. For me, this was normal Christianity. For me today, a man in my mid-thirties, it still is.

Church Shouldn't Suck...the Life Out of You is as practical as it gets when it comes to applying the hard-learned lessons of my father's life as pastor of The Harvest Church. Yes, that's right—I'm a preacher's kid and the oldest of five siblings. Our childhood was filled with the head-scratching, sidesplitting, and often unbelievable stories that are told in this book. And I swear that they are *all true*. I'd be the first to tell you if they weren't. As I first read through the manuscript of Dad's book, I thought to myself, *Why would anyone care to hear these stories that have been told and retold in my family so many times that all my siblings can relay them verbatim?* But as I saw them pieced together in a single manuscript, what emerged was not just a collection of one family's war stories but rather a testament to the power of simple obedience.

There is nothing heroic about my father, our family, or our church; we are not profound theologians. But growing up, I remember hearing over and over again that the only Jesus that so-and-so might ever see was the Jesus in *me*. That was a pretty heavy concept to drop on a seven-year-old kid, but to this day, it is our *modus operandi*.

I distinctly remember standing beside my father at about the age of eleven in a packinghouse in Palmetto, Florida, and being elbowed away from the conveyor belt by some very focused ladies as they picked out the imperfect vegetables so that we could use them to feed the hungry at our food bank. That day, I understood what the gospel was all about. I think it's telling that ever since then, all five of my father's children have worked with him side by side in ministry. That's quite a legacy. Thankfully, there are no more trips to the conveyor belt to fight for produce as we have found less combative ways of securing fresh vegetables for the food pantry.

This book is life-giving in that it gives every believer—from pastors to regular folks sitting in the pews—the liberty to simply be whoever God has called him or her to be, and to leave behind those things that have sucked the life out of church and the Christian walk. You should be having fun in church and in your walk as a believer. There should be a joy that springs up from the inside because you are doing those things that make you feel most fulfilled. Another great thing about this book is that it emphasizes the fact that there are no "style points" in the Christian walk. The journey is sometimes messy, sometimes heartbreaking, and sometimes frustrating, but there is a great reward in finishing the race.

So, if your church experience has been sucking the life out of you, grab hold of this book like you would a life preserver, and know that you're not alone—we've all been there.

Read it for your church; read it for your pastor; read it for yourself.

—*Jim Minor Jr.*
Associate Pastor, The Harvest Church
Sarasota, Florida

ON PASTORING AND POULTRY

I've been a pastor for a long time. Looking back, I can truly say that I've done it right—and done it wrong.

The best way to illustrate this anomaly is with an example. There was a time in my ministry when most of the people I was trying to reach didn't have their own means of transportation, so I actually had to go out and "round them up." My wife, Peggy, and I had this old station wagon, and I would drop her off at church and then drive the streets of Sarasota, Florida. I would make several trips back and forth, picking up five or six people each trip. At that time, these folks made up the largest part of our congregation.

Each Sunday was an adventure; I never knew who was going to show up.

On a typical Sunday, I might find Gregory, who had been hit by a motorcycle while walking down a railroad grade and had been in a coma for a time. Then he developed a drug problem, which made him shake continually.

Perhaps I would come across the toothless lady from West Virginia. She used to call me at two in the morning (yes, in those days, I actually gave my home phone number to anyone who wanted it), and she would say, "Pastor!"

I would answer, my head all groggy, "Yes?"

And then there would be silence.

Again I would say, "Yes?"

"Pastor!"

"Yes?"

"What'cha doin'?"

And that was it. Sometimes we'd do that two or three times a night, but we never got any further than "What'cha doin'?"

Some mornings, I would come across Cooper Cow. Cooper had a heart as big as anything, but he had the mental capacity of a twelve-year-old because he had been beaten severely with a pipe when he was young, in a case of mistaken identity. In the eyes of the world, Cooper was a "throwaway." He wandered the neighborhoods, and everybody knew him, but nobody really talked to him, because he would just nod his head and shout "Bang-Ar!" After I got to know him, I found out that what he was actually saying was "Praise God!"

There we'd come—me, a broke pastor in a broken-down station wagon, along with shaking Gregory, the no-teeth "what'cha doin'?" lady from West Virginia, Cooper Cow, and anybody else who happened to be walking the Sarasota streets and was brave enough to jump aboard. We'd arrive at our destination, head inside, and then, along with Peggy and some other faithful folks, we'd have church.

It was about this time that I really felt God calling me to start a food bank in order to feed these people, but there was no way we could afford it. Peggy and I had a hard enough time feeding ourselves and our four kids. But we were determined that we would begin to follow the call of God and see what He would do.

We obtained permission from some local farmers to "glean" their fields—to pick up the produce, such as tomatoes, cucumbers, and peppers, that were left after the harvest. Peggy and I, along with a few others, would work in the fields, fill up our station wagon with a variety of veggies, and bring them back to the church, where we would give them away. It's funny, but when our kids were growing up, they just thought it was a normal thing to dig around under the car seat and pull out a green pepper. They probably thought those grew there.

Because I was a broke pastor trying to minister to a broke congregation, finances (or the lack thereof) eventually forced us to change locations, and God placed us where we are now, on Lime Avenue. It's considered a pretty rough section of Sarasota, but at the time, it was right in the midst of the people we were trying to reach. I saw it as a blessing, because I wouldn't have to drive as far to pick up the members of my congregation. Around this time, Peggy's father passed away and left us a little money. Since we had outgrown the old station wagon, we splurged on a used passenger van. It was by no means new, but for us, it was plenty nice, and Peggy was thrilled because there were no vegetables under the seats—yet.

One day, I was at the church with a man named Jim, who often helped me with the food collection and distribution, when Gregory showed up and said, "Hey, Pastor, I know where we can get some meat."

This was a big deal for our little food pantry because we never had any meat. "Really?" I asked him.

"Yeah!" Gregory said, shaking a little. "I can get us some chicken."

By this point, I started getting excited. "Hot dog!" I said, and tossed him the keys to the "new" van. Meanwhile, I took the old station wagon to run some errands.

Later in the afternoon, I came back to the church, and as I rounded the corner of the building, the first thing I saw was a huge blue tarp hanging from the trees. The van was parked there with the back doors wide open. I went to close them, not wanting the interior lights to drain the battery. When I looked inside, I saw that all the rear seats had been taken out, and the back was piled high with crates—crates full of live chickens! That's right—the inside of Peggy's "new" van was covered with feathers and chicken poop.

I started screaming at Jim (forgive me, Lord) to get those chickens out of my van. Frantic, he began pulling out crates and putting them on the ground. My head was starting to spin. Then I quickly became concerned about this mysterious blue tarp hanging in the trees. Against my better judgment, I pulled back the tarp and took a peek. There stood Gregory with a young, scantily clad woman. She was obviously homeless, obviously drunk, and held two of the biggest knives I'd ever seen.

"She told me she's a butcher, Pastor!" Gregory said, with a big smile on his face.

They had set up a fifty-five-gallon drum half full of water, boiling from the roaring fire underneath. And the trees—oh, man, the trees—they were completely filled with chickens. Not live chickens, mind you, but plucked chickens—dozens of them—everywhere. Those poor chickens had had their head and feet cut off, had been boiled in water, and now were hanging in the trees outside my church.

I was frozen and speechless.

Gregory said, "I told you I was going to get some chickens."

"Chicken!" I screamed, my voice suddenly returning. "You said we can get some *chicken*! Not 'chickens'!"

I couldn't stand to look at it any longer. I turned and staggered back around the tarp, only to bump into—who else?—a City of Sarasota police officer.

"So," he said, trying to look around me and see past the tarp, "what's going on?"

For a half second, I considered tackling him. Instead, I just stood there as he stepped forward and pulled the tarp aside. There was Gregory, shaking back and forth; there was the drunk girl (the "butcher") with the huge knives; and there was Jim, looking guilty and wide-eyed, holding a crate of live chickens.

I watched the cop as he took it all in. I saw him slowly look up into the trees at all those bald, headless chickens. You must understand that our church was still pretty new to the neighborhood. I could only imagine that this poor cop thought he had stumbled upon some sort of cult animal sacrifice ceremony or something.

Finally, he stepped back and, real cool, asked, "Who's in charge here?"

I'll be darned if all three of them, without saying a word, pointed right at me! I want to jump up and down and scream, "I just showed up! I didn't do anything! I thought we were getting wings and drumsticks and stuff. Look at my wife's van! It's full of chicken poop! She's gonna kill me!"

But nothing came out. I just stood there.

"Look," the cop said as he turned around and started walking back to his car. "You can't have an open fire like this in the City of Sarasota. You need to put it out."

I nodded, closed my mouth, and motioned to Gregory. He decided that the quickest way to get rid of the fire was to kick over the fifty-five-gallon drum. As he did, boiling water ran across the ground, scalding the feet of all the live chickens still sitting in the crates. Man, did those birds go absolutely wild! "WAAA-BAAA-BAAA-BAAA!"

At this point, Jim and the knife-wielding drunk girl were dancing around to avoid the boiling water, while Gregory continued to stand there, shaking like a leaf. All the chickens in the crates were still going crazy. I just had to turn and walk away.

On a side note, I later learned that those chickens were so shocked that they laid eggs. The reason Gregory had gotten them from the farmer in the first place was that they had quit producing eggs. Who knew that if you poured a little hot water on their feet, they'd start dropping eggs like crazy! We eventually took the remaining chickens to a pastor friend in Palmetto. He kept them for at least five years and said they were the best egg-laying chickens he had ever had.

Here's the funny part of that story: It took place during a time when I was pastoring the *right way*.

I know what you're thinking: *Holy cow, Jim. If that's what you looked like when you were doing it right, I'd sure hate to see you when you were doing it wrong!*

Well, let's talk about that. How do we know when we're pastoring the right way?

And more important, you might ask, "If I'm doing it wrong, what does it take to change? Is it absolutely necessary to have dead chickens in my trees? Because I don't know if my people would go for that. I run a pretty respectable church, you know?"

Relax.

PASTORING THE PAINFUL WAY

Pastoring the wrong way has absolutely nothing to with what kind of bird is in your trees, or whether the birds are alive or dead. Pastoring the wrong way has everything to do with *pain*. In case you haven't figured it out yet, pastoring can be incredibly painful.

A few years ago, a gentleman came to The Harvest. Like many others who show up at our church, he was in rough shape. He had no money, no place to stay, and no fight left to battle the alcohol and drug problems that tormented him. We admitted him to the Harvest House, our live-in rehabilitation ministry designed to help men battling addiction to get their lives back on track.

Over the next few months, I loved all over this guy, and I really got to like him. We hung out together while the campus on Lime Avenue was undergoing renovations, and he helped us with odd construction jobs here and there. He would use my pickup truck to haul away junk or to pick up materials from the supply house—whatever needed to be done. The reconstruction of church and man alike progressed slowly, but before long, both were looking good. My friend was staying sober, keeping clean, and getting his life back on track.

Until the day he didn't come back with my truck.

That hurt. I mean, I really liked that truck, you know? But, while that situation didn't work out the way I would have liked, on the PPS (Pastor Pain Scale), it was pretty small. In fact, if losing a nice (did I mention it was really nice?) pickup truck was the greatest pain I ever had to endure in more than thirty years as a pastor, I wouldn't have felt so strongly about writing this book.

But the fact is, in trying to fulfill God's calling on my life, I have encountered some major pain. Real pain, not just the had-my-pickup-truck-stolen sort of pain. In fact, a year or so later, that guy showed up again, beaten and broken and crying, and I hugged him, and we tried it again. And, no, he wasn't in my truck. He was on a moped; he had totaled my truck in Ohio.

When it comes to real pain, I can vividly recall seasons of pastoring when every day brought with it a stomach-turning anxiety of just waiting for the next terrible thing to happen. Whether it was a financial hardship, the politics of running a church, or just the day-to-day curveballs we all experience, I can remember thinking, *What else could possibly go wrong?*

Don't ever ask that, by the way. It's not helpful. Because, sure enough, every time I allowed myself to ask that question, the train seemed to jump off a set of tracks that I hadn't even known it was on. I remember sometimes closing myself in the office, sitting real still, and asking God, *If this truly is a mandate from You, if this truly is Your work I'm doing, then how can it possibly be so fragile? How come it seems like the whole thing is going to fly apart at any second?*

I can tell you that the worst thing about trying to fulfill your calling while dreading every moment is that it quickly sucks the life right out of your ministry. When that happens, you no longer have the energy or the fight to stay engaged, day by day. As bad things come (most of which involve people), it's only a matter of time before you start to harden and become jaded, even to the point where—holy cow, am I saying this already, when we're only in chapter one?—you find that you can't stand to be around the very people that God has called you to serve!

Let me be very clear to each member of my lovely church family who may be reading this book: I don't mean you. I mean those *other* people.

Seriously, I had to learn that the most difficult thing about being a pastor is not coming up with a good sermon. It's the fact that people—yes, even Christians—can sometimes be cruel. It's the Moses experience: Today, you are the people's deliverer; tomorrow, they want to stone you. And when I was pastoring wrong, I didn't know how to deal with that. I knew I couldn't quit; I was doing what I was called to do. I loved pastoring. It just so happened that some days, I really couldn't stand people.

Over time, I started ministering from a distance. I was no longer leading with my heart. Walls went up. I told myself that in my position, it was a necessary thing to be guarded, even distant. Eventually, however, I looked around and realized that I had ordered my life in such a way that I no longer had any truly close friendships—deep relationships with people who had full access to the hidden places of my heart.

In fact—and it hurts me deeply to admit this—there were times when even my family didn't like me all that much. I had missed so many birthdays and anniversaries and family meals that I had succeeded in placing them at a distance, too.

Am I striking a nerve here? Does anything sound familiar?

I hope so, because here's a truth: When our loving Father calls us into the privilege of serving His precious children, what I've just described is nowhere close to what He had in mind. Nevertheless, I believe that there are many good people in ministry—pastors and laypeople alike—who find themselves stuck in this exact spot. They're not done with their calling, by any means, but they sure are sick and tired of "doing church as usual." For these folks, more days than not, the job of doing ministry really *sucks*. And by that, I mean that church is sucking the joy and purpose right out of life.

Many pastors have worked themselves into the place where their ministries have become just another job, leaving them to wonder if this is all there is to their calling. They no longer experience the heart-swelling, head-spinning passion that first caused them to forsake all and follow God. The fire of the love affair with ministry they experienced in their youth is gone. They pour themselves out until they are dry, merely going through the motions. They continue dutifully operating their ministries, but they've put up walls that hide their feelings of emptiness. After years of giving it their all, many have reached a season where the joy of their ministry is all but buried beneath the drudgery and meaninglessness of their jobs. Some have convinced themselves that the true rewards for their service will come later, and that God requires them to hang in there and keep trudging along until they reach the "great by-and-by." Some have concluded that hanging in there is simply not possible, and they are considering leaving the pulpit; some have even turned to distractions of the flesh in order to compensate for the dryness of their duties.

They have forgotten their first calling—a love affair with Jesus Christ.

Some of you are laypeople who serve in ministry but are bored to tears because you feel like a hamster on a wheel—working hard, exhausting yourself, and getting nowhere. You thought you'd be serving the hurting and lonely, but you feel like you are serving only your pastor's ego by helping him to build a bigger and bigger organization. You feel guilty for wanting out, but you dread each time you must go to church to "serve."

Others of you sit in the pews of zombie churches—congregations that died and lost the heartbeat of the gospel a long time ago but continue to stagger along. Somewhere along the line, you just accepted the fact that church is supposed to be boring—that's just the way it is, so you might as well get used to it. Or perhaps you've already reached the end of your rope and have left "organized religion." You'd happily go back, if only there was meaning and purpose and adventure to be found in "doing church." If only it made a difference in the world, you'd move heaven and earth to be a part of it. If only...

I am here to tell you, as a man who has crossed that "sea of lies" and come out on the other side: It doesn't have to be that way. It's not *supposed* to be that way. Pastoring doesn't have to be painful. It doesn't have to be lonely. Christianity was never meant to be boring. Faith was never meant to be fruitless. There is another way.

PASTORING GOD'S WAY

In these pages, I am going to be as open and honest as I possibly can about the things I have learned during my many years as a pastor. I'm going to talk about doing it wrong, and I'm going to talk about doing it right. I am going to try to reach the hearts of the men and women traveling along the same path I was once on, in hopes of preventing them from stepping into some of the same messes that I did. At some points, I will be specifically addressing those who have the job of pastor; at other points, I'll be addressing all frustrated Christians. But I truly believe that we can all benefit by speaking the truth and seeking a better future for the church.

Along the way, I am also going to ask you to be willing to question some of the things you may hold dear. I may offend some of you, and that's okay.

I, too, was once easily offended, but I got over it.

AND THE GREATEST OF THESE...

In order to minister effectively, we have to love. We have to love beyond our personal limitations. We have to love beyond our firmly held beliefs. We have to love beyond our religion.

A little while ago, I was talking to a good friend of mine named David, who was relating an incident that occurred at a local hardware store. As he was heading out the door, an old farmer was coming in, dressed in overalls and covered with dirt. With each slow step, the old farmer's face would tighten and twist. He would take a step and curse. Another step, another curse. As they passed each other, David asked the farmer how he was doing. The farmer fired back, "I'm just #@%!! fine!"

My friend asked if there was any way he could help, and the farmer stopped and leveled him a cold stare. "My #@%!! hip hurts," he blurted out, "and that's about all there is to it."

Well, David is not easily put off. He asked the farmer if it would be okay if he prayed for him.

"Sonny, if that's what the #@%!! you feel like you need to do, then you just go right ahead."

And so he did. Right there in the doorway of the hardware store, David prayed specifically for healing in the farmer's hip, and he laid hands on him in the name of Jesus. When he was done, the old farmer turned to walk inside the store, and David continued to his car.

After a few steps, however, he heard the farmer yell, to no one in particular, "Hey! How about that!"

David turned around and watched as the old man shook his foot and shifted his weight from one leg to the other and back again.

"Well, I'll be," the old man said, never looking back. "That feels pretty #@%!! good! That feels better than it has in #@%!! years!" And with that, he continued into the store.

I share this story because, for years, that episode of the farmer, and other ones like it, just didn't mix with my theology. It didn't sit right with me that God would heal a man who would so blatantly take His name in vain, who wouldn't even acknowledge that his healing had come from God, or who didn't display the right amount of faith. I thought that, as a pastor, I had figured out all the conditions that were necessary for God to show up and do His thing. I never would have stated it that way, but looking back, that's exactly what I thought. By introducing all my own requirements into a situation, I had placed strict limits on what God could do and when He could do it.

CHECK YOUR FOCUS

I used to notice that "the farmer"—representing everyone like him—was not attending church, when I should have been agreeing that God desired for him to be healed. If "the farmer" didn't display what I considered to be the proper amount of faith, I would allow that fact to trump the truth that God's love conquers all. I would listen to my own pet traditions and give credence to all the reasons people told me that healing would not happen, completely overlooking the fact that God desperately *wanted* to heal this man, and He wanted to use me to do it!

Instead of focusing on God and fighting the battle on His terms and by His rules, I was completely wrapped up in my own beliefs and distractions.

By focusing on my traditions, my religion, my expectations, and my definition of God's love, I had completely tied His hands in the battle He had laid out for me. No wonder I wasn't seeing many miracles. Instead of agreeing with God that a miracle could happen, I was spending most of my energy rehearsing all the reasons that it probably wouldn't.

Thankfully, the kingdom of God is on a forceful advance, and it marches on, despite my screwups. In fact, God loves me so much that He is forever calling me to refocus only on Him—putting everything else aside, looking into His face, and experiencing His love. My Father tells me, time and time again, "I don't want your religion. I don't want your tradition. I don't want your firmly held beliefs. I just want your heart. I can do amazing things if you'll just give Me your heart."

Too often, our good-intentioned efforts to protect the good name and good image of our good Lord actually handicap us in the battles we are called to fight. This only distracts us from what really matters and prevents us from fully loving the people—all of them unique images of God—that He has placed right in front of us. By giving heed to our messed-up thinking, we essentially remove ourselves from the battlefield—the really tough, hard frontline stuff. We shirk our responsibility to be used by God, saying things like "Only God can heal," or "Only God can change a heart." We lose sight of the fact that God wants to do these things *through us*. His design for the growth of His kingdom is for the miracles to serve as confirmation of His Word. His heart is for the sick and the poor and the broken, and when we take care of the least of those among us, we are taking care of Him. (See Matthew 25:40.) Sadly, it seems that the Western church has become more focused on church expansion and internal programs for those who already profess Him as Lord than on truly taking new ground for the kingdom of God.

And this is a tragedy, because Jesus is not coming back to heal the sick; He is not coming back to cast out devils. Instead, when He returns, He is going to look around and see what we did with what He placed in our care. He left it to us to heal the sick, cast out devils, and spread the gospel to the ends of the earth, and He fully expects us to do so. He said,

> I *will give you the keys of the kingdom of heaven, and whatever you bind on earth will be bound in heaven, and whatever you loose on earth will be loosed in heaven.*
>
> (Matthew 16:19)

This verse states that Jesus has given us the keys. What an interesting picture! Have you ever seen folks who think they're important because of all the keys they carry? They walk around with a big ring of keys; sometimes, they even hook on more rings so they can collect more keys because it makes them feel important. I always wonder if they even know what all those keys go to, and if those people ever actually open anything. Now, don't get offended and throw down the book if you've got a lot of keys. I'm just saying that keys, by themselves, aren't important, and we shouldn't be satisfied just to possess them.

USE THE KEYS YOU'VE BEEN GIVEN

Jesus Christ has given us the keys to the kingdom of heaven, but not just so that we could carry them around and jingle them in front of people. He didn't give us the keys so that we could attend pastors' conferences and compare the number of keys we carry. God gave us the keys to the kingdom of heaven for one reason: *so we could use them.* We have the power to release heaven—love and healing and deliverance—to a hurting world. Desperate people are knocking on the door of the kingdom of heaven, and all of us who call ourselves Christians have the keys that will open it to them.

We are not called to determine who "deserves" entrance to the kingdom and who doesn't. We are just called to use the key. We are not called to discern if it is in God's timing. Just use the key. We are not called to decide who is worthy to carry the keys and who is not. Just use the silly key already!

Too often, we focus on everything but the fact that the authority of heaven, the blessings of heaven, and the joy of heaven are prepared and ready. God is a *right now* God, and He is available to everyone *right now*, including the crusty old farmer. That's why he received his healing right there in the front entrance of the hardware store. He wasn't required to first stop swearing or to go to church or to be baptized or to repent or to have enough faith. He was able to be healed simply because my dear friend did not hesitate to use the key that Jesus Christ had given him—the very same key that He has given to you and to me.

When we, as pastors or laypeople, surrender all the other silly things we allow to consume us, and begin to focus on unlocking heaven, our calling no longer feels like a job or like drudgery. We stop worrying about building a success-ful ministry, because we understand that it's God's responsi-bility. We don't spend endless hours debating money issues with our church committee, because when we begin to oper-ate in line with God's vision, He gives us the provision. We no longer wonder how to get the people sitting in the pews truly excited, or why so many miracles seem to happen in Third-World countries but not in the United States, because excitement and miracles are an integral part of unlocking heaven.

The hard truth is that it's not God who's holding back healing and deliverance and the next great wave of revival; it's the church, with its screwed-up mind-set. It's about time that we stop leaning on tradition and religion, stop treating the kingdom of God like a business, and, for heaven's sake, stop blaming the farmer!

Mankind is groaning, and it's time for the church to be the church. It's time to unlock heaven.

The kingdom of God is on a forceful advance, with or without us. If our relationship with God has grown dis-tant, or our ministry for Him has grown stale, then we need to rediscover our first love. Unloading all the garbage that He never intended for us to carry is the first step toward our return to the front lines of the battle, the place where His heart's desire resides—out there with the hurting, the hungry, and the desperate. God is longing to use us in ways we never dreamed possible, but He doesn't want our preconceived ideas of how that should look to get in the way.

God has called us to a wild and wonderful ride, but we can't bring our baggage. All we can bring is our love. *"And now abide faith, hope, love, these three; but the greatest of these is love"* (1 Corinthians 13:13).

CHURCH AS USUAL

Let me back up a bit and tell you how I came to reach that perfect pastoring plateau of chickens in the trees.

In my early days of ministry, I often felt conflicted, perhaps due to the fact that I was trying to follow a ministry course that had been spoken over me. A godly influence, someone I truly considered to be a prophet, had given me this word: "Even though you came from a difficult background, you are now middle-class, and that is where you will find your success. You will build a great church by reaching out to the middle class."

This excited me because, growing up as a punk kid in Long Island, New York, I was definitely not considered to be "middle-class." I married way up when I married Peggy, and it excited me to hear this word because, at the time, I took it to mean that I had *arrived*. It caused me to anticipate the financial aspect of my life becoming easier and more affluent. So, I owned that prophecy. I claimed it. I worked to build my congregation, pouring everything I could into it, and eventually I arrived at a point where our church was rolling along—we were growing, tithe money was coming in, and the bills were getting paid. But despite how well things were going, the whole thing began to seem rather hollow. I knew God had more in store for my life. He simply had to, because He is not an unfulfilling God.

Deep inside, I felt this urge to reach out to the poor and the broken; but every time it surfaced, I would remember the prophetic word spoken over me, and common sense would kick in: *If I do that, who's going to pay the bills? Poor and hurting people don't have any money; they* need *money! I have to focus on the people who have money. When I have that extra cushion, then I'll start ministering to the poor.*

Man, I was miserable.

At times, I even "ran away" from church. As often as I could, I would head down to the worst neighborhoods in the inner city and minister to every poor and broken and down-and-out person I could find. When I was in the heart of the ghetto, reaching into the lives of the people there, I was truly at peace. I was filled with joy.

But, sooner or later, I would have to drag myself back to my church, back to my "job," where, sure enough, a cloud would settle over me.

Peggy and I had built our church from five people to about two hundred people over a span of four or five years. People would come and people would go, but there was no real glue; most of the people seemed to be drifting through. We had a nice middle-class congregation, we were growing and paying our bills, but there was no fire, no breath of God.

In fact, I felt that I was closer to the heart of God when I was out on the streets with the homeless than when I was standing in the pulpit on Sunday morning. If you asked me to pinpoint, during that season, exactly when the Holy Spirit of God was flowing the most freely, it would *not* have been during Sunday services. So, I have to ask: Was I really giving the people in my church a chance to experience God? Or was I only giving them a good sermon?

I guess the sermons were okay, because the place filled up each week. Good people came to hear me preach, and we offered them good parking and good programs for their kids and a good message. The whole thing was…good. We had settled into doing church as usual. And it was so incredibly painful.

A BASIC COMMAND

Years earlier, Peggy and I had spent time at a church in Miami that had been truly experiencing the touch of God. They were out in the streets, caring for the hurting and the broken, taking ground for the kingdom, and literally transforming the city. They were really making an impact in the community for the gospel.

Over time, however, they grew to a certain point, bought a lot of acreage, and built a school. When this happened, they made the decision that they really didn't want to do street ministry any longer, because they didn't want their brand-new school to be exposed to the dirtiness that comes with street ministry.

When that happened, the fire of God left that church, and so did we.

Now, here we were Sarasota, in almost the same boat. We were reaching the middle class, running what the world would call a "successful" church, but we were ignoring one of God's most basic commands: Feed the hungry. And while our church was in no danger of going out of business, the hard truth was that the business of God was being ignored right outside our front door.

Think about this: It would be ridiculous to build a church without the intention of spreading the gospel. Spreading the gospel of Jesus Christ is one of the cornerstones of the Great Commission. As Christians, we would not stand for a church in which a bunch of people gathered together without the express intent of leading people to the saving power of Jesus Christ. We would not put up with a church that went out into the neighborhood only once in a while to tell one or two people about Jesus. That would hardly qualify as "spreading the gospel," and it would be questionable if we could even refer to that as a "church." We spread the gospel because Jesus Christ commands us to do so. It is one of His most basic commands for His church. It is one way we can do the works that He did, only greater. (See John 14:12.)

In the same way, feeding the hungry, clothing the naked, healing the sick, and caring for those in prison are cornerstones of being a Christian. In the book of Matthew, Jesus Himself let it be known that this was how He would differentiate between the sheep—those who would be invited to share His inheritance—and the goats, or those who would be turned away because of their unfaithfulness.

Our salvation is not based on our works but on our accepting the work of Christ Jesus on the cross. Nevertheless, Jesus makes it clear that works *are* expected of us. Remember, faith without works is dead. (See James 2:20, 26.) As Christians, we are expected to take care of the least of humanity—of those who bear His image. That is love, and we are called to love. If we ignore or merely pay lip service to this most basic command of the gospel, we are shrugging off an essential part of our calling. Telling lost people about the saving grace of Jesus Christ is an essential work of the gospel, but so is loving those who bear His image.

It is a fallacy that "certain people" are called to take care of the hungry and the broken, just as it is untrue that only "certain people" are called to spread the gospel. These are basic commands for *all* Christians. I was being torn apart inside, because, in my belief that I had been "called" to minister to the middle class, I was living out this conflict of trying to create a successful church at the expense of doing what God truly wanted me to do.

In my church, as in many other churches, there was a direct call from God that was not being answered. My wife watched this for years and finally had the wisdom to let me know that I was "doing it wrong." I had been allowing the perfect will of God to lead my heart when I was out in the streets but paying Him mere lip service from the pulpit on Sundays. And while the things that I was preaching to my congregation were true, I wasn't sharing the entire truth of what God had called me to do, all because I feared that they would run off if I did. I was trying to do church without doing the complete will of God.

That's what it took for me to finally realize that a good, godly person—someone whom I considered to be a prophet— had just missed it that day. He had given me a good word, but it was not God's best. Doing church as usual was causing me to miss what the kingdom of God was all about. The double-mindedness was not satisfying to me; in fact, it was sucking the life right out of me.

When I finally stared straight into the true calling of God and accepted it in its entirety, not just the spreading-the-gospel part, it was very liberating. Lights came on. Chains came off. There was an incredible peace as I began to rest in His direction for my life instead of my own.

Joy returned to my life, as ministry no longer felt like a job.

DISCERNING GOD'S WILL— AND GOING "DOWN"

While I would love to tell you that it was all gravy from that point on, that would be a lie. In fact, my first hardship came right away, when I went to my congregation and told them, "Get ready. Get prepared to greet somebody who doesn't look like you or smell like you. Get prepared to sit next to somebody who may have urinated on himself or hasn't showered in a month. We are going to the hurting and the afflicted. We are going to reach out to the broken, to those nobody else wants."

Of course, everybody left.

Well, almost everybody. I saw my church congregation decrease from hundreds of people to fewer than forty members. Most of the congregants didn't buy in to the new vision because there was nothing anchoring them to our church except the trappings of convenience—good music, good programs, halfway decent preaching, and the fact that we were located close to their homes and always let out on time.

The hand of the living God was not holding them; the hand of man was. And when we removed that support— when the structure went out of services and the prettiness went out of church—they quickly left to find someplace else that was more convenient and better suited to their vision of how church should look. That may sound harsh, though

I don't mean it to. After all, it wasn't their fault; it was mine. I had built a congregation on my own abilities and my own ideas of what would be best, rather than chasing the true call of God, even though I knew that was right. I had built a middle-class, people-pleasing church, and when the people were no longer pleased, they scattered.

The best thing I ever did was lay down my ideas of how to build a successful church and instead run with God's idea of success. As long as I labored to build my church the best way I knew how, there was no joy in my ministry. True, I had built a successful "business model" of a church. I was the CEO—the guy in charge of what type of people showed up, what they were exposed to, and exactly what time they got out. My focus at that time was entirely on the church— the bride of Christ—rather than on Jesus Christ Himself, and I was exhausted. As a result, the pews were full, and the bills were paid; but I was miserable because I knew I wasn't experiencing God's best. By leaning on my own abilities and accepting only a portion of what He had called me to do, I had limited what God actually *could* do through me.

Consequently, like many pastors and other church leaders today, I had built a church of spiritual consumers. By holding myself responsible for every aspect of the service— the music, the message, the schedule, the attendance—I had decided in advance when and how God could show up. My concerns were all about the program, and God had simply become another part of that program.

But once I dropped that model, it was incredibly liberating, because I was finally where God wanted me to be. There was absolutely no way I could pay the bills; in fact, every weekend when five more broken (and broke) people showed up, it seemed that ten people who had been faithful tithers would disappear. But I knew it was the right thing to do; I knew it was going to work out, because, for the first time, it wasn't up to me to build my church. It wasn't my plan; it wasn't my responsibility. I had given that to God. It was His plan, and He was responsible for making it work. I was staring at Him, no longer paying attention to what kind of people came through the door, and certainly not worried whether or not they had money. That was His problem, and you know what? He handled it.

I have to admit that it didn't look anything like how I would have done it, or even like I had imagined it. In the beginning, to the outside world, we appeared to be a huge failure. But I knew I was in the right "field." I had this picture that God had called me to pick beans, and that's where I was—right in the middle of the bean field. I wasn't off in the middle of the watermelon patch trying to pick watermelons and getting frustrated because God wasn't blessing my harvest.

More important, I no longer felt like I was just doing a "job." I had been called to a great work, a mission; and although it was difficult at times, it never felt like a burden. I guess that's what convinced us that we were on the right track. Even though ministry became incredibly difficult, it was pure joy. We were alive. Yes, a large portion of our congregation left. But God began to show up because we were walking out His plan, not ours. We may not have had all the outward appearances of a "successful church," but when we began to reach for broken and hurting people in a real and meaningful way, we touched God's heart. And that is true success in ministry.

Do you know what? Life is better these days. When it comes to being a pastor, I chase the things that are close to

God's heart, not mine. I focus on God and let Him worry about growing His church. Every now and then, I might have some chickens in my trees, but that's okay, because the joy is back in my ministry.

I am in love once again.

Church may not always be convenient for the people who come to The Harvest, but it sure is more rewarding. Everyone suffers for doing church as usual, but when we open our eyes to everything that is on God's heart, those in the pulpit and pews alike are more richly blessed as a result.

CONVENIENCE

When you're a pastor, your heart yearns to reach the multitudes, but when you are doing church as usual, you always have this message of convenience ringing in your head: *Don't keep the congregation in the service too long. Don't sing too long. And, for goodness' sake, don't preach too long! Don't ask them to change. You're lucky to get this little slice of time out of their busy week, so make sure you don't blow it. After all, there are so many other churches they could choose, and you really want them here. You really need them here. In fact, attendance needs to increase a little more so that you can do all those things God wants you to do. So, don't do anything stupid, like look them square in the eye and tell them that you want their money; after all, there are so many other churches they could be attending instead. You're lucky they chose to be here. That new place around the corner just added a brand-new gym, and there's even a Starbucks in the lobby. A Starbucks! I wonder if we could do that....*

The church that is focused on convenience will never know the fire of God. The fire of God falls on sacrifice, not on convenience. The powerful, life-changing presence of God does not settle on your congregation because you open a new gym or give away free coffee or begin a new singles' program.

I'm going to make some of you mad. Get ready.

In a typical church today, there are programs for teens, preteens, seniors, married couples, singles, and on and on and on. Many pastors and staff members are just flat worn out because it's one program after another. That is not Christ's design for the church; that is man's design to make church "convenient" by catering to the needs of everyone. It's a competition to pack the pews, because only then will there be a certain number of tithers who will contribute a certain percent of their income, which will make it possible to build that new gym so we can offer that basketball program that will make it more convenient for parents to bring their children, which will result in a certain number of tithers who will contribute a certain percentage of their income, which will make it possible to...I think you get the picture.

I have nothing against gymnasiums and coffee and programs, until they start distracting us from the work that Jesus Christ has called us to do. When the church leadership adopts a mind-set that says, "The purpose of this program is to make things more convenient and attractive for our guests," it will encourage a mind-set on the part of the congregation that says, "I choose this church because it offers me the most conveniences."

THE DANGERS OF INSULATION

Many of the people who have stopped coming to The Harvest over the years left because we did not provide the "perfect program" for their kids. In truth, I suppose it is possible that some left because we occasionally have dead chickens hanging in the trees. Nevertheless, a great number of well-meaning parents have had as their primary concern the "perfect program," usually defined as one that would insulate their children from the harshness of the world while also teaching them about God's love for those who are caught in it. From where I stand, these parents actually do their kids a great disservice in neglecting to prepare them for the spiritual battle that is adolescence.

This is horribly sad to say, but some of the kids whose parents left in search of the "perfect environment" ended up returning to our church later as members of our drug rehabilitation program. We actually wound up counseling young people whose parents wouldn't allow them to come to The Harvest for fear of exposing them to the very things that those kids went on to experience anyway.

My son Dan, who serves as the assistant pastor at our church, talks about this paradox of going to church and being confronted by the darkness versus going to church and being insulated inside the "perfect program":

> Every kid gets to the point where he begins to question the bill of goods his parents are selling him: *Is this God-thing real, or is it just a way for my parents to get me to stay out of trouble?* I believe that even before I reached that age of questioning, I had been confronted with enough concrete evidence to convince me that the power and presence of God was not only real but was also capable of dramatically changing a person's life.
>
> I didn't grow up insulated from the reality of the darkness or, more important, from what happens when the presence of God confronts that darkness.

Even as a young child, when I walked past someone in the ditch, I knew that God could use me to have a profound effect on that person's situation because I had grown up watching the same thing happen, time and again. As a result, I eventually came to see every man in the ditch as my obligation.

The amazing power of Jesus Christ to conquer drug addiction, alcoholism, and other demonic strongholds was something I was intimately familiar with, as was the damage these strongholds could wreak in a person's life if they were not confronted. I didn't need school to teach me that drugs were bad. I witnessed it.

Thus, part of the process of becoming an adult was evaluating what I'd been told versus what I'd seen with my own eyes, and when I did that, there was no other option as to how I was going to live the rest of my life. I had seen too much. I knew God was for real.

THE PITFALLS OF CATERING TO EVERY PREFERENCE

Not every "perfect program" in the world will open the heavens. The heavens open when we touch the heart of God. Is God concerned about teens and seniors and singles? Yes, of course. But too often, the church looks at these groups as people to minister to rather than seeing them as people who should in turn be ministering to others. Because of this competition among churches to make these groups feel loved and appreciated, many pastors are afraid to ask them to do the very thing that would fulfill them the most: actively and purposefully love those who bear God's image.

As a result, the burden of satisfying these people falls on the pastor and church staff members, who become incredibly worn out trying to keep everybody happy and content. Many of those who try to fulfill this impossible task eventually come to see the calling of God on their life as a job and a burden. The fire for ministry goes out—or, at the very least, grows dim.

Moreover, churches that overload themselves on programs inevitably feel the need to add staff members. In order to successfully serve all of these various groups and subgroups, they require a pastor to seniors, a pastor to singles, a youth teen, a children's pastor, and a pastor to old women who love to knit pot holders. Salaries are huge drains on church budgets. This bloating of the church payroll then requires churches to work even harder to attract the "right people" (those who tithe), resulting in a demand for still more programs. It's a vicious cycle that completely takes the focus away from those who don't bring in the cash—the hurting people out there in the community—and places it internally, on regular church attendees who are already "in the fold."

Is there such a thing as a good program? Yes. Programs edify the body of Christ when their purpose is to facilitate encounters with God and to make Him a reality in people's lives. This happens when the goal of the program lines up with Jesus' goals for the church: Go make disciples. Go feed the hungry. Go reach the hurting and the broken. When the program's sole purpose is to make life easier for the parents, pacify their children, or increase the church rolls so that everybody feels good about what he's doing, things begin to go off track.

The way to measure the success of a church program is to assess its ability to transform a city. Is the darkness being pushed back, or is the light of God shining only within your church building? The Bible says that we should not put our light under a bushel. (See Matthew 5:14–16.) All the joy, all the love, and all the light that God gives us should be used in pushing back the darkness and taking ground for the kingdom, not by perpetually washing our own feet. Out there, outside our church walls, a battle is going on—a battle that Jesus has called and equipped us to fight. In most cases, sadly, that battle is raging no more than a few blocks from our parking lot.

Which brings me to this: The church that Jesus Christ envisioned should be shocking people with its outreach. If our own neighborhood is not constantly being amazed by the things that our church is accomplishing through the power of Jesus Christ, then there is little of value that we are offering the people who sit in our pews every week. Most things that happen within the walls of the Western church, whether it's the seniors' baking ministry or the men's volleyball team, never surprise anyone.

Building a gym in order to get kids off the street and teach them about Jesus Christ is a fantastic thing. It needs to be done. But it's only half the program. When we think like Jesus and come in line with His vision for the church, we will send those kids back into the street to serve their fellow man. They will be actively involved in sharing the gospel, feeding the hungry, and helping people get delivered from bondage.

The first option is child-centered, the second is Christ-centered. The first may touch a kid's heart for a season, but the second will touch God's heart and have eternal consequences.

GOD'S CHURCH GROWTH PLAN

In the end, we really don't need programs to attract people to our churches. It may sound crazy, but *it's not our job to attract people to our churches*. The attraction to church should be the joy, the fire, and the breath of God that people experience when they come there. It should be the miracles, divine healings, deliverances, and salvations that are taking place. After all, this was God's original plan for how to pack a church: Miracles were to serve as confirmation of the Word being preached.

GROW A CONGREGATION OF GIVERS

The church that Jesus Christ modeled is not a church of *consumers* but rather a church of *givers*. Too many Christians have become consumers of spirituality, because too many churches have allowed themselves to become religious Wal-Marts. They have placed themselves in competition with the church down the street to offer the most consumer-friendly Sunday experience.

Like any other business, some churches are very good at this—they attract many customers. Others are not as good and go out of business. As in any other enterprise, courses are charted and decisions are made based on the happiness and comfort of the people sitting in the pew. In this age, churches are predominantly white, predominantly black, predominantly Hispanic, and so forth. We have churches divided by age, socioeconomic spectrum, and musical preference. One of the main reasons for this is convenience. Different people may fill the pews for different reasons, but many times, convenience is what keeps them there.

Too many Western churches are built by man, for man.

We have churches that start out with the business plan of becoming the next megachurch. When I look at the structure of how they are put together, I see that it is based around the idea of catering to those who attend: offering the best programs, the most convenient location, the finest amenities, the easiest parking. Mix in some inoffensive preaching with a highly structured program that always lets out on time, and what more could people want? It is a perfectly pleasant place to pay your weekly diligence to God.

But while these churches might be able to draw a bunch of folks, no great harvest—no great move of God—is going to come of it. The message of the hour is not a message of convenience but rather a message of giving your life away. The model of the effective church is not one where the person sitting in the pew is the ultimate beneficiary. While believers will benefit immensely, they do so by presenting themselves as tools that God can use to bless their community and world.

As leaders of the church, we sometimes become wrapped up in the belief that the success or failure of a church depends solely on *our* efforts. We forget to include the power of God in our growth plan. Unfortunately, when we start with a self-oriented viewpoint, we end up with a self-oriented church.

GROW A CONGREGATION THAT TOUCHES GOD'S HEART

The success of a church depends on how it touches God's heart, how clearly the people see His vision, and how completely they move in it. While a consumer-oriented church might have a good financial bottom line, when preaching, programs, and punctuality are substituted for the power of God, is any lasting good really being accomplished? Are we truly pushing back the darkness, or have we simply become a spiritual country club with a great day-care program?

To be the church that Jesus envisioned, we need to call forth the sick and the hurting during our services. When they come down front, we need to pray boldly over them in the power and authority that Jesus Christ has given us. We need to use the keys He left to His church. When blind eyes start seeing and deaf ears start hearing, when broken lives begin to mend and marriages are restored, people won't be coming to church looking for a program for their kids; they'll be seeking out the power of the living God!

Jesus wanted the church to reach out to the broken, to continually take ground for the kingdom. That was His commission: "*Go…*" (Matthew 28:19). And as the people went into an area, they understood that the reason for them to establish a permanent presence there was to reach the people locally, beating back the darkness right there in that city, in that neighborhood.

Today, there are definite, aching needs within the very neighborhoods where we pastor, and we cannot be so nearsighted that we see only the people who show up at our particular Sunday services. Our obligation to serve goes way past Sister Martha in the front row and the occasional visitor who wanders in. God is calling believers to go rub shoulders with the people in their city. He is calling pastors to go out and pastor their whole city. It absolutely breaks His heart when we step over the man in the ditch on our way to "have church."

It is vitally important to give the people sitting in our church pews a solid spiritual foundation, but it is dangerously shortsighted to focus solely on them. As spiritual leaders, we do God a great disservice when we turn the bulk of our attention to our congregation, because that automatically puts us in competition with the congregation down the street. Every Sunday becomes an arms war, a battle to get them to come "here" instead of "there."

GROW A CONGREGATION WITH GLOBAL FOCUS

The church that Jesus Christ envisioned is a worldwide network of people, all laboring for the advancement of the kingdom of heaven. It is not a building on the corner with a sign out front that continually feuds with the building on the next corner with a different sign out front. For us as the church, our passion should be about transforming our city, which means that we should also support other congregations that have the same mind-set. After all, we are not in competition with other bodies of believers—we are teammates, fellow soldiers, in a battle against the forces of spiritual darkness. In every community, the church has an obligation to discern and battle the darkness and the strongholds that are trying to destroy people's lives.

The Bible says, "*Unless the* LORD *builds the house, they labor in vain who build it*" (Psalm 127:1). When a church is not about doing the things that touch God's heart, it doesn't invoke His presence. And when His presence is not there, neither is His miraculous provision. As the pews fill up, the church might have plenty of money, but if God is not building the house, all the labor is for naught.

A church that is focused on pleasing its people will eventually die.

A dead church is not necessarily one from which all the people have left; it's one where God is not moving in a real and powerful way. It is a house without His presence and without His provision. It is a house where decisions, whether big or small, are made based on revenue. New programs are created with the main goal of retaining the people who currently populate the pews. Outreach is designed with the idea of expanding church membership rather than touching the heart of God.

Love is overruled by the line-item budget.

If we are aiming for the ideal tither on whom to build our church, that's exactly what we'll get: tithing money. But if we are actively and purposefully dedicated to reaching the poor and the broken, if we truly reach for the heart of God, then the heavens will open. We will stop operating on a monthly budget and begin operating under an open heaven.

GOD'S VISION BRINGS HIS PROVISION

As a rule, when we are busy doing the things that God is involved in—things that are close to His heart—it places us smack-dab in the midst of His presence; and, consequently, it invokes His provision. This allows us to do things that are beyond our natural reach and outside the means of our visible resources. As a layperson or a pastor, the moment we look at what we have, in the natural, and allow that to determine what we are going to do, we're in trouble. Relying on the external appearance of our situation closes off any hope of supernatural provision.

At The Harvest, we witness God's miraculous provision on a daily basis. Quite simply, the things that God does in this house are not possible based on the natural.

We are a church of about four hundred people. If you visit our church on any given Sunday, you're as likely to sit next to a county commissioner as you are to sit next to someone who was recently released from jail. Actually, that's not true…you're *way* more likely to sit next to someone fresh out of jail.

If you decide to visit us a second time, you're officially a member.

Many of the people in our congregation are current or past participants in Harvest House Transitional Center, a subsidiary of our church. Harvest House offers a wide range of human service programs, including the Freedom and VETS programs, which offer residential substance abuse treatment to ninety-eight men, women, and homeless veterans; Alive Again, transitional and graduate housing for our Freedom program participants; and Home Again, our newest and fastest growing program that provides housing and intense case management for chronically homeless families with children. Harvest House, along with its low-income housing programs, has a capacity of three hundred eighty beds each night. We work with all of our program participants, helping them get back on their feet after dealing with legal issues, drug or alcohol addiction, homelessness, or any one of a million other things life has hit them with.

These programs do not provide merely a bed for the night or a meal for the day. They are long-term, live-in programs designed to reestablish people's footing on the firm foundation of the love of God. We feed them. We help them find work. We provide day care, transportation, and medical care, if needed. But mainly, we just show love to people who haven't experienced love in a long time. We allow them to believe that they *are* lovable, that they are *worthy* of being loved.

In addition, we operate the following ministries from our Sarasota campus:

- Free Indeed, our in-house food bank, which supplies a week's worth of groceries to more than 250 local families every Thursday.

- Harvest Prayer House, where more than two dozen men and women trained in the *Sozo* method of healing and deliverance (more on that later) donate their time to provide free sessions of in-depth prayer for anyone who may need them.

- Acts 5th Avenue, which provides clothing, shoes, household goods, furniture, books, toys, and other essential items to families in need. If you can pay, that's fine; if not, that's okay, too.

- M28 Ministry School, a two-year program focused on equipping students to fulfill Jesus Christ's vision for His church.

- Low-cost housing that is purchased, renovated, and made available to those who qualify.

- An in-house media ministry that recently produced *Living Proof*, a twelve-episode documentary on gaining freedom from addiction, scheduled to air on GospelTV throughout Europe.

- We cosponsor an off-site ministry school in a facility that we purchased and renovated. This two-month live-in program trains future missionaries to go forth and claim nations for the kingdom of God.

- We recently funneled more than one hundred thousand dollars to foreign missions supporting an orphanage in the Dominican Republic and a Bible College in the Philippines, and we sent a container of 10,000 pairs of shoes, a huge tent, and 50,000 meals to Africa. (More on that later, too.) Recently, we were able to purchase and renovate thirty-eight additional local housing units.

I mention all this to brag on God. It's obviously all Him, because there is no way we could have come anywhere close to doing all of this with the money we take in. The math simply doesn't add up in the natural world. In God's kingdom, however, under an open heaven, it makes perfect sense.

OBEDIENCE INVITES MIRACULOUS PROVISION

After one of His sessions of preaching, Jesus told His disciples to feed the large crowd that had gathered there to listen to Him. His instructions stumped the disciples, because they had only a small boy's lunch of five loaves of bread and two fish. In the end, five thousand men had eaten their fill, and there was even food left over. (See, for example, John 6:5–13.) The feeding of the five thousand is often used to illustrate how Christ can accomplish a lot with just a little, but I think that this teaching misses the major point.

Jesus was also sharing with the disciples with His plan and vision for what He wanted to accomplish: "Feed the people!" The disciples watched as Jesus thanked His Father for the food, and then they distributed it until everyone had enough. It was indeed a miracle—a small boy's lunch had fed five thousand men, plus women and children. God had worked through His Son, who was fully man, to multiply the food to the point where every need was met, and there was more food left over than what they had started with.

Everything Jesus did was an example of how we, as His followers, should walk on earth. It's all about fulfilling the will of the Father. God is ready to use our hands to feed the hungry exactly as He used Jesus' hands to feed them. God's heart is for the hungry to be fed—that is His vision.

To accomplish His vision, He will always provide the provision.

IGNORING YOUR NATURAL EYES

As the church, we simply need to operate in that reality rather than act according to what we see with our natural eyes. If we begin to move, God will provide the means. After all, it is His will that is being accomplished, not our own. It is His vision and His plan, and He will make sure that it comes to pass.

None of the ministries I mentioned that we launched made any logical sense when we started it. We looked at what God had called us to do, we looked at the resources we had on hand, and then we looked at each other and said, "That's too big. We can't do that now."

There was never enough money, never enough time, never enough manpower available. And yet, God always made a way, because these were things He wanted to see accomplished. They were things that touched His heart, and as we jumped in and got started, He sent the provision we needed. He miraculously multiplied what little we had in order to accomplish His goals. We simply had to keep our focus on Jesus Christ and His vision rather than on our available resources. We had to believe that what Jesus told us was possible rather than what our circumstances told us was possible.

At The Harvest, since we are after the things that touch God's heart, we operate under an open heaven. He is our Source. We never look at numbers on a page in order to determine if we can move forward; we just stay focused on what God tells us to do. Our job is to see His vision and to walk toward it; His job is to provide the means to get there.

Because we are the church of the Creator of everything, our decisions should never be based on money. Money is such a fickle thing, such a shaky foundation, to base our actions on. To create a budget based on the funds that came in last month, and to allow that number to be the main determining factor in what we are going to do next month, completely shuts God out of the process.

To count our money, look at our options, chart our course, and then ask God to bless it is walking forward in the power of money rather than in the power of the Almighty. It is placing our faith in the manna rather than in the One who provides it.

STEWARDSHIP GOD'S WAY

At one point in His ministry, Jesus was asked whether it was right for God's people to pay taxes to Caesar. (See Matthew 22:15–22.) This gets right to the heart of the issue, which is: How should we handle money? Today's churches struggle with money issues more than anything else. They deliberate over such questions as these: Should we add a new program? Should we make a new hire? Should we construct a new building? Should we increase our missions giving?

To answer the question about taxes, Jesus turned the inquiry around, forcing the questioners to examine their own hearts. He said, *"Show Me the tax money....Whose image and inscription is this?"* (Matthew 22:19–20). When they replied that the money bore the image of Caesar, Jesus instructed them to render unto Caesar that which is Caesar's. (See Matthew 22:21.)

How do we know what belongs to Caesar? We know it does if it bears his image. That which bore Caesar's image had the power to buy things in the kingdom of Caesar. It was the currency of the Roman Empire. If you wanted a donkey or a home or food, you simply had to take care of your money. That which bore the image of Caesar worked in the economy of the natural world, and even though the style of coin has changed, that truth still applies today. Take good care of your money, and you can enjoy all the things that money can buy.

But there was a second, more important, part to this story: *"Render therefore to Caesar the things that are Caesar's, and to God the things that are God's"* (Matthew 22:21). How do we know what belongs to God? Again, we know because it bears His image. And what is it that bears God's image? It isn't a coin or a mountain or a lake or even the stars of the sky. God put His image on something to declare that it belonged to Him—He put his image on mankind. Humanity bears the image of God. (See Genesis 1:27.) In the same way that taking care of that which bears Caesar's image brings you purchasing power in the kingdom of Caesar, taking care of that which bears God's image brings you purchasing power in the kingdom of God.

Caring for God's people racks up credit in the economy of heaven, where the world's financial rules no longer apply. Caring for God's people allows us to operate under an open heaven.

Let me give you an example. Eureka is the lady who heads up our Free Indeed food ministry. One of the many local organizations we support is an orphanage called Everyday Blessings. We typically provide them with food on a weekly basis.

One Thursday, Eureka came to me and said, "Pastor, [some people from] Everyday Blessings are here, and they are asking for things that we don't normally give them—things like toilet paper and napkins and paper towels. We have only enough of that stuff for the church to use. If I give it to them, we won't have any for the services this weekend."

I told Eureka, "Here's what I want you to do: I want you to go into the pantry and give them everything we have. Don't worry about what the church has or doesn't have. Let's just bless them. Give it all." Then I took her hands in mine, and we prayed and giggled a little bit, and said, "Let's just see what God does."

I was scheduled to be out of town for the weekend, so I went ahead and left.

When I returned on Monday, Eureka couldn't wait to talk to me. She told me that on Friday, she had received a call from someone saying he had some stuff he wanted to give to the church, but someone would need to bring a truck to pick it up. (Man, don't you love it when people say that?) Sure enough, when she got there with the church's box truck, the gentleman had a couple of pallets of—guess what?—napkins and toilet paper, enough to wipe every mouth and bottom in all of Sarasota County.

Sometimes, when God tells us to give freely, we think that it contradicts His message of being a good steward. It doesn't. Being a good steward of God's money simply means spending it when and where He says, rather than when and where we think we should. We don't push a roll of toilet paper on everyone who walks in our door, but when the people from Everyday Blessings showed up, one thing was certain: God had already revealed His vision for us to care for them. The fact that they came to our door and asked lined up perfectly with God's vision—so we didn't hesitate. We moved forward in His vision, and He provided the provision.

Right now, you might be thinking, *Jim, that's cute—you got some napkins. Tell me another funny chicken tale.* Well, hold on. Let me see if this next story gets your attention.

Our church also supports Iris Ministries, founded by Rolland and Heidi Baker in response to their calling to Mozambique, Africa. The last time they came to The Harvest, God really impressed on Peggy and me the importance of shoes to the people to whom the Bakers minister. Few people in Mozambique own shoes, and the result is that infection and disease are widespread. We had never considered the notion of blessing a population of people with footwear, but here was a situation in which God clearly revealed His heart. There was no question that we were to move in that direction, adopting His vision as our own.

I didn't go and ask how much money we had in the bank or how this could be worked into the budget. (They would have just stared at me, anyway, because we don't have a budget.) I didn't look at what we were currently spending and search for areas to cut back so that we could afford some shoes. In fact, I did not see myself at all responsible for the financial aspect of making this happen—the provision was God's job, not mine.

My job was simply to move forward in making God's vision become a reality. I presented the idea to our congregation, and within a few short months, we had purchased a forty-foot shipping container and filled it with more than 10,000 brand-new pairs of shoes. The provision for this effort was nothing short of amazing. We had people with next to nothing donate a single pair of shoes, and we had corporations like Skechers donating three thousand pairs.

In addition to the shoes (because God is a God of more than enough), we were also able to provide a new enclosed tent measuring 80 by 160 feet and 50,000 meals. We built the tent in our factory, and the meals were donated to the effort by Feeding Children Everywhere, based in Orlando, Florida.

When we began to move forward in His vision, God caused the word to get out, and before long, all kinds of people and organizations were asking what they could donate to send in our shipping container.

When we finally had the container loaded and about ready, there was still some room, so we started grabbing folding chairs from our church and clothes from our clothing ministry and whatever else we could find to fill it. We might have even stuffed a few small children in there who weren't paying attention—I'm not sure.

All in all, it ended up costing us about $40,000 to purchase the container, fill it with supplies, and ship it to Mozambique. The entire church caught the fire of God's vision, and it went from revelation to reality in an incredibly short amount of time. If we had been operating on a budget, obeying the laws of Caesar, we would have looked at this situation and agreed that somebody should do it—that it was a great cause—but, unfortunately, it just couldn't be us at this time.

Instead, the only concern we had was taking care of those who bear the image of God; and, true to His nature, He provided the provision to make it happen.

While all this was going on, we were also working with the local HUD (Housing and Urban Development) office, through their Neighborhood Stabilization Program, to acquire a number of properties in our neighborhood. As we mentioned earlier, our church buys run-down urban houses, renovates them, and uses them to either expand our rehabilitation programs or offer housing to qualified individuals with low incomes. This is part of the vision God has given us to transform our city. It is a way in which the church can go to the city rather than wait for the city to come to the church.

Anyway, the deal had been structured so that the mortgages on the properties totaled $2.5 million and were to be paid back interest-free beginning in thirty years. I was comfortable with the church assuming this debt, because thirty years would be plenty of time to establish cash flow on the properties. Besides, when thirty years were up, I'd be dead, and it would be my son's problem to deal with. (That was a joke we told at the time.)

We had just agreed to this deal on the homes when we found out that our shipping container was stuck in customs in Africa. The customs officials were demanding an additional $18,000 for its release! This was way over and above what we had figured, but Peggy and I agreed that we did not want Iris Ministries to incur any burden in receiving the blessing we intended for them. I told her that even if we had to borrow money on our home, we were going to cover the fee. We dug deep, we scraped, and we paid up. This wasn't one of those times when you find out you need $18,000 and you miraculously receive a check for that amount in the mail. No, this was one of those times when, in order to bless someone through us, God called us to go way beyond what seemed possible, way outside where we expected to go or thought we were capable of going, and really left it up to us to get there. And we did, barely. The container was finally released, along with the blessing that God had planned for Iris Ministries.

Shortly after this, I was sitting in my office when Laura, our church administrator, called me down to look at a letter we had just received from HUD in reference to the properties we had just purchased. In my mind, I was thinking, *Man, I sure hope this isn't about money.* Sure enough, it was. The letter from HUD said that they were sorry, but somehow they had misinterpreted the guidelines of the Neighborhood

Stabilization Program. The $2.5 million in mortgages on the properties would not come due in thirty years, as originally stated. In fact, it would not come due at all. The entire debt had been cancelled. "Have a nice day," the letter concluded.

Excuse me?

We had to call and verify that one. Sure enough, it was exactly as it appeared to be: God had wiped $2.5 million of debt off our books. Of course, the lady at HUD didn't credit the Almighty, but we knew better!

In these situations, and in many others over the years, we have caught God's vision and have received back in abundance. Our motive in giving was never to get; our motive was always to take care of that which bears His image. We gave all we had to Everyday Blessings because the children needed it, and it brought us abundantly more. We stretched beyond what we were financially able to afford in order to send shoes and a tent and meals to Mozambique, all because we were caring for His image-bearers, not because we expected the cancellation of a major debt.

We were simply sowing and reaping the currency of the kingdom of heaven. We were loving people. As God's church, when we take care of that which bears His image, we operate under an open heaven. We should never sacrifice taking care of those who bear God's image in order to take care of that which bears Caesar's image.

CHURCH SHOULDN'T SUCK

On the side of the truck we use for our food ministry, we painted a caricature of a man's face getting sucked off by a vacuum cleaner. Over his head, in big blue letters, it proclaims: "Church Shouldn't Suck."

It never fails to get a response.

In fact, our drivers have been accosted countless times because of that van. Just the other day, Eureka was taking a load of food to our satellite church in Bartow when she noticed that the woman in the next lane was white-knuckling her steering wheel while screaming out the window.

This dear lady followed Eureka to a gas station, where she proceeded to give her a tongue-lashing about how to be a better Christian. She had opinions about the truck, about our church, about me, the pastor, and even about Eureka, who just smiled and invited her to join us for worship on Sunday. Eureka later remarked that while this lady may not have been a joyful Christian, she was at least passionate.

In all seriousness, the fact that we even felt the need to paint that phrase on the side of our truck shows how short the church has fallen in its aim to represent the true Jesus. As a society, we have *churched* ourselves into a corner, where it often seems our first order of business is to refute all the horrible perceptions that other people have about us.

This begs the question: When we look at the average church in the U.S. today—not your church, of course; just the average church in the average town—can we say with certainty that it exudes a love, a joy, and a peace that attracts the world? Is the church attractive to the world around it?

As we've already discussed, I'm not talking about whether it's convenient or whether it's located in the right section of town or whether it meets at the right time and offers the right programs for my kids. You're probably thinking, *Please don't get started on programs again.* What I mean is this: Are people drawn to the church like metal to a magnet; like a bride to her true love?

I believe the answer depends on whether the Holy Spirit is present and in charge. If so, when people come in, they will be accosted by a spirit of love, and there is nothing more attractive than love. In fact, no matter what people might think they're coming to church to find, love is the only thing that will truly satisfy their souls. And when love, in the Person of the Holy Spirit, is allowed and encouraged to flow freely, the house will be full of life. People will sense that there is something inside those church doors that they can't find anywhere else in the world.

There is another major advantage of turning over our services completely to the workings of the Holy Spirit: It ensures that religion and tradition are not in charge. *Religion* is church done by man; *tradition* is church done by man in the way his fathers did it. Both methods create a dead church quicker than we can point out a speck in our brother's eye.

EVERYTHING DEPENDS ON THE PRESENCE OF THE HOLY SPIRIT

The Holy Spirit is the power of God to save someone to eternal life. The Holy Spirit is the love of God to restore broken hearts and homes and marriages. The Holy Spirit is the life of God that causes people to worship their Lord with everything that is in them, rather than just clapping politely when a song is finished—if clapping is even permitted!

As pastors, we can stand up in front of the church and read directly from the book of Hebrews, and every bit of what we proclaim will be true. It will be the letter of God, the living Word, pure and unadulterated. But if, in delivering our message, we restrict the free movement of the Holy Spirit, it will be a lifeless sermon.

Stay with me here; don't throw away the book just yet.

When the living Word of God is delivered through a lifeless vessel, there won't be any life in it. Any subject from the Bible—salvation, deliverance from demon possession, blessings and prosperity, whatever—can have the life sucked completely out of it if it is delivered through dead bones.

Our ministry is written not with ink on tablets of stone but with the Spirit of the living God on the tablet of the human heart. (See 2 Corinthians 3:3.) Therefore, we cannot allow ourselves to stand in the pulpit and simply administer the letter of the law. We cannot be satisfied to have a form of godliness while we deny the power thereof. (See 2 Timothy 3:5.)

If we deliver merely the letter of the law, we will constantly try to bring the people to the letter by holding it up and saying, "This is where you're wrong! This is where you need to change! This is why things are going wrong in your life!"

Under the new covenant, we in the pulpit are charged with bringing the Spirit of God, not the law, to the people. In order to do this, we must give the Holy Spirit free rein in our services. As pastors, we must allow the Spirit to take charge, and we must not become offended when He changes our plans. We must not be resistant when He gives us a different message to preach from the one we have prepared, and we must not grow anxious when He wants us to worship for a longer period of time than what is "normal." Above all, we must not hammer people over the head with a bunch of rules and regulations. God loves His people with an incredible love, and that is what they should experience when they come into His church—His love. When the Word of God is delivered with life and with love, people are drawn to it. They want to touch it, taste it, and see that the Lord is sweet. (See Psalm 34:8.) Sure, the truth may sometimes sting a little, but it is sweet above all. It is attractive. It draws us in. It should never repel.

This living love can be poured out only through a vessel that is filled with and yielded to the Holy Spirit. If we, as pastors, are not completely yielded to the Spirit—if we are insistent on always delivering our predetermined message, maintaining our perfect schedule, and hammering people over the head because "we love them so much"—then we are delivering only the letter of the law, and we should not be surprised when nobody is drawn to it.

If you are a Christian layperson who has left the church because you were led to believe in an angry and vengeful God, I can say only this: You were fed a pack of man-made lies. The divine truth is that God is not mad at you. He is reaching out to you like the father of the prodigal son (see Luke 15:11–32), yearning for the day you return to His house so that He can love you as His dearly beloved.

Unfortunately, far too often, we have allowed the life-giving Spirit of God to be sucked out of our churches, leaving behind nothing but dead bones. As pastors, we have delivered only the lifeless letter of the law. The result is that the people in our pews feel nothing but condemnation. Meanwhile, the outside world looks in our doors and says, "Man, I don't want any of that!" Think about it: When people come to church, how much guilt and condemnation get heaped on them? When they sit in the pew and listen to all the "Thou shalt not's," do they feel any love at all from the One who created them?

I have actually heard people express the desire to be saved the day before they die, but not a day before. Isn't that sad? They know they need a Savior, but they don't want to "waste their lives" on religion. I don't blame them! And it's not their fault; it's our fault. If that is the impression people have of church, then, somewhere along the way, we've done church a disservice. People are simply not attracted to dead bones.

Recently, a new church opened near us, and some of our Harvest House guys went to check it out. Now, keep in mind that every one of these guys has tattoos on his body and years of hard living on his face. The group of them came back and told me, "Pastor, they looked at us like we were criminals. It was pretty obvious we weren't welcome there."

I happen to know that all of these men are on fire for the Lord. They have seen Him do incredible things in their lives, and they each have a mind-blowing, miraculous testimony of the restorative power of Jesus' love. These men should have been welcomed in with love and rejoicing, but instead they were given a forced smile and a chilly attitude.

In the end, love cannot be faked. And when those on-fire, sold-out-for-the-Lord, Jesus-loving men left that church, they couldn't escape the impression that it had, for lack of a better way to put it, sucked.

We need to reject the mind-set that says that anyone who doesn't fit the profile of our congregation must therefore be bad or undesirable. The Bible tells us that Jesus wasn't much to look at; there wasn't anything overly impressive in His outward appearance. (See Isaiah 53:2.) He spent His time in fellowship with sinners, not with saints. (See, for example, Luke 15:2.) Churches need to establish an atmosphere in which every individual is seen as a reflection of the image of God. After all, each of us has our own dirt; some of us just hide it better than others.

Another time, a lady from the streets with some mental problems came into our church. We were in the midst of a prayer meeting, interceding on behalf of others for certain things. People were on their knees or lying on the floor, spread out all over the place.

This lady got up and started walking across the tops of the chairs, pointing at people, and saying, "Duck, duck... goose, goose...duck, duck...goose, goose!" Finally she got to one guy and said, "And you're a son-of-a-b----!"

She just kept going, row by row, walking along the chairs and saying, "Duck, duck...goose, goose!" Every now and then, she'd yell, "You're a son of a b----!"

We're used to seeing strange stuff at The Harvest, but the poor ushers didn't know what to do with this lady. To complicate matters further, she was rather scantily dressed, and they either couldn't or wouldn't grab her to restrain her. So, she just kept on going. I positioned myself at the end of a row, and when she got right next to me, I stood up, threw her over my shoulder, and headed for the door. She kicked her legs while still pointing and ducking and goosing all the way outside.

Sure, some people may need to be shown the door—with love. But do you know what? That woman is welcome back to The Harvest anytime. And who knows? She just might show up, because she certainly didn't think our church sucked—she was having a ball!

WHO IS WELCOME?

That was a drastic example, but we truly need to ask ourselves who, exactly, is welcome in our church and who is not. Is the man who has gotten divorced welcome in our church? What about the man who is married to a woman of a different race? What about the man who was just released from jail for beating his wife? Which of these individuals would Jesus turn away rather than welcome into His house?

What about the man who is addicted to alcohol, or the man who hasn't had a bath in weeks? Will we hug them and love them right where they are? Or will we require them to clean up the outer man before we accept and love the inner man?

What about the man who wears clothes made of animal hair and eats wild bugs? Is there a place for John the Baptist in our church? (See Matthew 3:4; Mark 1:6.)

Religion sets up all sorts of guidelines to make a person look better, act better, and smell better. It is completely concerned with the outward appearance of a man. There is no love in religion; its "love" is conditional, based on a person's adherence to the established religious guidelines. Religion believes that when the heart of a person is right, he should look, act, and smell a certain way. Therefore, rules are set up defining how people should look, act, and smell. The intention is to make a person *appear* pure in heart without having to do the dirty work of actually reaching his heart and purifying it.

Religion creates churches that are whitewashed tombs, full of dead men's bones. (See Matthew 23:27.)

The true love of God, in the Person of the Holy Spirit, is the only thing that will bring life and joy to the church. We must see other people with God's eyes, not with religious eyes. Yes, people are broken and hurting, but we must love them to wellness, not condemn them to stay sick.

While religion wants to prune every branch that is not perfect, the Holy Spirit urges all to stay connected with the Vine and to submit themselves to the Vinedresser's loving care. He will take care of the pruning. (See John 15:1–2.)

BUT WE'VE ALWAYS DONE IT THAT WAY!

When it comes to restricting the Holy Spirit in our services, religion has a twin brother: tradition.

Tradition can be recognized by a concentration on keeping things as they have always been rather than yielding to what God is trying to do at the moment. When they hear the word "tradition," we tend to think of the old-line churches with their tall stained-glass windows and monk-like priests walking up and down the aisles chanting things in Latin.

While this is definitely church in its most conventional sense, we can miss the fact that many modern, Spirit-filled churches also struggle with the roadblock of tradition. In fact, some churches have seen great moves of the Holy Spirit in terms of miracles, healings, and deliverances, and this can make them reluctant to move on and find out what God has in store for them next.

Some churches become obsessed with recreating the exact conditions that led to a past move of God. They believe that whatever conditions constituted the "perfect place" at one point must be maintained. They think to themselves, *The music was exactly like this, and the message was exactly like this, and our hair was big and our suits were brown, so we need to go back to that time and stay there!*

The truth is that as soon as a moment becomes a movement, it's on its way out.

When the Israelites were wandering around in the desert, following the presence of God in the form of a cloud by day and a pillar of fire by night (see Exodus 13:21–22), their guide sometimes moved and, at other times, stayed still. The people knew to stay put when God stayed put, but they also knew that it was time to move when God moved.

I can imagine a couple opening up a bagel shop during one of the periods in which God's presence stayed put. This couple worked hard and had a fantastic, booming business until, one day, they went to work, and no customers showed up. They couldn't figure out what went wrong. They were still making the same bagels and delicious coffee they had always made; they were still offering the same friendly service as always. Nothing had changed. Yet their customers had disappeared. They decided to stick it out for another week to see if things would improve. No change. They stuck it out another week. And another. But their little shop never came back to life.

What happened? The cloud had moved, and they hadn't gone along with it!

God is a progressive God, and as His followers (as in, those who *follow* Him), we have to accept and understand that God moves on. If something was working yesterday but isn't working today, we need to believe that God is leading us on to bigger things.

Does this mean we throw away everything that He has ever revealed to us in the past? Absolutely not. But instead of planting ourselves in place and trying to recreate a past moment, we need to take those lessons with us and build on them. Every move of God is meant to bring us closer to His heart and to prepare us for what is next.

For example, when the Holiness Movement, which focused on right living, gave way to the baptism of the Spirit, we were not supposed to throw away all the blessings we had received before. The resurgence of speaking in tongues and the exercise of the gifts of the Spirit were to go along with what we had learned from the Holiness Movement—an understanding of right living, repentance, and sanctification. They were not meant to be a replacement.

Unfortunately, many young people walked away from what they saw as their parents' movement and pursued the baptism of the Spirit, while many of their parents resisted the new move of God. In fighting to hold on to the fire they had experienced in the Holiness Movement, those parents eventually caused the whole thing to become focused on outward appearances only. What had started as a beautiful outpouring of God dealing with internal issues of the heart, such as repentance, prayer, and a pure walk, eventually came to be about wearing the right clothing and hairstyles and jewelry. The fire of God had moved on.

While God is progressive and always advancing, His gifts are timeless. Even though we don't wear the same styles (hopefully) or worship in the same way we did during the peak of the charismatic movement, we are not called to toss aside the wonderful moves of the Holy Spirit that happened during that period. By allowing the movement to keep advancing, we watched the gifts of the Holy Spirit revive Presbyterian, Catholic, and Lutheran churches alike. We witnessed the birth of the entire messianic movement, in which Jews were filled with the Holy Spirit.

Unfortunately, however, we also have many churches that are still trying to start a fire with the ashes of past outpourings. At one point, they were in the middle of a great movement of God, but now, when they try to recreate the exact same conditions again, the whole thing comes off as lifeless.

In some places in the U.S. today, one can find thirty elderly people worshipping in buildings that used to host thousands. The next generation is nowhere to be found. These are good people who sincerely love God, but their pastors haven't allowed them to follow the harvest. They are stuck in a place where God really moved for them at one time, but because they have limited God to that single outpouring, they are missing all the blessings that God had in store for them next.

I guess the message that the body of Christ needs to hear is that we really *can* take it with us. We really can take what happened in yesterday's outpouring and carry it with us wherever God wants us to go today. And when He has someplace new for us to go tomorrow, we should be ready and willing to move. We don't want to be the guy in yesterday's brown corduroy pants and platform shoes, waiting in vain for God to show up in power like He did so many years ago.

EYES ON CHRIST

The relationship between the prophets Elijah and Elisha in the second chapter of 2 Kings portrays the relationship between Christ and the New Testament church. Elijah represents Christ, while Elisha, his protégé, represents the church. When the Lord was about to take Elijah up to heaven in a whirlwind, Elisha (the church) requested from Elijah (Christ) that he might inherit a double portion of his spirit. In turn, Elijah (Christ) said to the Elisha (the church), *"You have asked a hard thing. Nevertheless, if you see me when I am taken from you, it shall be so for you"* (2 Kings 2:10).

The church is called to perform even greater works than those that took place during Jesus' earthly ministry (see John 14:12), and to accomplish that, we are given a double portion of His blessing. But the critical thing for us to do, as the church, is to *see* Him. We have to be constantly looking toward Jesus Christ with all our eyes, all our minds, and all our hearts.

We cannot focus on the moves of yesterday or on any of the other trappings of religion and tradition that seek to divert our attention. Only by looking continuously at our Lord Jesus can we be assured that we are standing in the present move of God. Only then can we be certain that we are not sitting around a campfire that has gone out, fanning the ashes of past outpourings.

Staying focused on Jesus, and on what He is doing now, guarantees that we will never find ourselves stuck in an out-of-date, powerless form of religion.

THE PERSON IN THE PEW

There can be no real growth, no forward movement, in the kingdom of God until the person sitting in the pew gets excited—until he believes that God has a personal calling on his life and that the advancement of His kingdom on earth depends directly on his actions. The highlight of his spiritual walk should not be showing up on Sunday morning to "consume" church but rather going out into his city, Monday through Saturday, to *be* the church. In order for this to happen, he must be convinced that God has a direct role for him to play.

I can hear pastors screaming, "Yeah, you tell 'em, Jim!" Well, hear me out and then decide if you still agree with me.

Many times, we pastors create an atmosphere in our churches that actually holds the congregation back. As we discussed previously, by doing everything we can for the convenience of the people in the pews, whether it is catering to their schedules, bowing to their musical preferences, or granting their individualized program requirements, we can foster a mind-set in our congregants that causes them to see themselves as consumers.

The inherent danger in this attitude is the underlying separation it causes within the church itself. When people get the impression that the church exists to serve them, it only follows that there will be one group of people (the church staff) whose role it is to minister to others, and another group of people (the congregation) whose role it is to be ministered to.

Since American society is so consumer driven, this mind-set has proven successful in packing the pews of many churches across the nation. However, if we uphold this mind-set, we are not being honest with our flocks about the responsibility to which Jesus Christ has called them. Bill Johnson, senior pastor at Bethel Church in Redding, California, puts it this way: "Jesus came to destroy the works of the devil, and He said to you and me, 'As the Father sent Me, I send you.'" (See John 20:21.)

It's important to understand that Jesus was not exclusively addressing pastors or those holding an office in a fivefold ministry—apostles, prophets, evangelists, pastors, and teachers. (See Ephesians 4:11.) He was talking to *all* Christians, from the person in the pulpit to the man or woman in the last pew. As pastors, our job is to train people to go into the world (starting with their neighborhoods) and destroy the works of the devil.

ALL ARE CALLED TO GO

Think about this: In many churches, more than half of the men or women sitting in the pews are not confident in their ability to lead a stranger to Christ. In many cases, they would be far more comfortable inviting that person to church and letting the pastor handle it. "After all, that's his job!" they say. As pastors, we would hope that our congregants would be better equipped than this, but we must consider whether we are part of the reason they are not.

The responsibility for growing the kingdom of God rests mainly with the "average" man and woman sitting in the pew, and our calling is to equip these saints so that they might do the work of the ministry. Unfortunately, we in the pulpit can get so wrapped up in the Sunday-morning service that we forget the fact that most of life happens Monday through Saturday. We can become so focused on delivering a compelling church experience that we expect our congregation to live for Sunday morning, too. Our entire concentration goes toward getting our message just right, and we gather around us those who can get the music, the multimedia presentation, the Sunday school, and everything else just right. Then we feel victorious when Sunday morning goes off without a hitch—when everyone comes in, gets "churched," and gets out on time.

Unfortunately, this mind-set creates a situation in which some Christians are viewed as the "working" part of the church—those who make it happen—while some see themselves as the ones for whom church happens—they are the "audience" for our "show." One image to illustrate this better is that of a train, with one or two locomotives pulling hundreds and hundreds of cars. As pastors, we must reject the notion that our job is to pull our congregations along. Their walk with God should not be coupled to our spirituality or the lack thereof.

As part of the fivefold ministry, members of the clergy are called to serve the body of Christ by empowering the saints.

Our greatest responsibility to the people under our care is to teach them that the Holy Spirit will propel each of them down the track that God has called him to under His power, not our own. The growth of the kingdom is built upon the work of the saints, most of whom will never be called into the traditional fivefold ministry. In this paradigm, the Sunday-morning service becomes the "huddle," preparing God's team to go into the world and run the plays Monday through Saturday.

If you think about it, this was Christ's original plan for the church—not that a few men would sit around a church building and evangelize whoever happened to drop by, but that those few men would empower a city of ordinary people who would, in turn, evangelize the world. As pastors, we can get so wrapped up in our position of influence that we forget to do our job. We are here to serve the people who sit in the pews, and that goes way beyond doing whatever it takes to entice them to come back the following Sunday or to compel them to contribute to the offering, whether that be free coffee, good day care, or a feel-good message.

Our best efforts at doing "church as usual" fall far short of God's plan for our congregations. And if we take our pastoral callings seriously, somewhere along the line, this responsibility of fulfilling the gospel message must be passed on to our congregants. They must understand that they are called to their own personal love affair with the King of Kings, and that they have a personal responsibility to advance the kingdom. They need to get out and be the church, but that can't happen if we don't train them, encourage them, and release them.

ANSWERING THE CALL

Awhile back, a young lady named Misty visited our church and told us that God had called her and a few other women to begin meeting with people and, in her words, "just let the Holy Spirit show up." The meetings involved everything from spiritual healing to physical healing to spiritual warfare. In the past, they had struggled to find a location to meet, often being forced to hold meetings in their cars. Even though she had attended services at The Harvest only a couple of times, she felt led to ask if they could use a small room in the church fellowship hall during times when it was open.

We discerned immediately that God was in this young ministry, and we gave Misty a key to the church, telling her it would be available whenever she needed it. She had come out of a much more controlling spiritual environment and was astounded that we would do such a thing. She asked, "Don't you even want to know what we do?"

We told her, "Not really; just do whatever God calls you to do."

About the same time, my wife, Peggy, and I were in Africa, and she received word from the Lord that she was to bring "*sozo*" to the church. At that point, she had no clue what *sozo* even was. In researching it, she discovered that it was the name of a healing ministry through Bethel Church in Redding, California. *Sozo* is a Greek word often translated as "saved," "healed," or "delivered."

Bethel had developed Sozo as an inner healing and deliverance ministry aimed at restoring and completing a person's connection with the Father, Son, and Holy Spirit, believing that with a healed relationship with God, people would be able to walk in the destiny to which they had been called.

It seemed a natural fit for the ministry that was already operating in our fellowship hall, so we came together with Misty and asked her to prayerfully consider it. Today,

Harvest Prayer House has over two dozen volunteers ministering to people every week, helping them gain freedom from bondage and fulfill God's plan and purpose for their lives. As a pastor, I am thrilled that this ministry operates on our campus and that our people feel empowered enough to step out and minister to others without having to check with church leadership before every session.

Harvest Prayer House has grown into something that amazes all of us, and the reason is that we let God take the helm. Someone sitting in the pew believed enough in the call of God to become active, and, as a church staff, we didn't tie her down with all sorts of made-up qualifications and conditions; instead, we simply trusted God and released her to fulfill her calling.

God gives everybody certain gifts and callings, and the gifts of the Spirit should be flowing through the hairdresser and the auto mechanic as easily and effectively as through the pastor and other church staff members. An on-fire, devil-chasing, Jesus-loving hairdresser can have as great an impact on a city as a pastor can—maybe even greater! The majority of people in any given area are not going to walk into the four walls of our church, but if everyone who comes to our church goes through the week with the gifts of God supernaturally flowing out of him, imagine the impact that it would have on the advancement of the kingdom! The pulpit ministry exists for one purpose alone: to perfect the saints to do the work of the ministry.

It gets ugly, however, when we pastors limit the ways in which our congregants may serve because we fear that our position may be threatened otherwise. We subconsciously hold back our people by limiting their service to God to those things that we think will help our own Sunday ministry profile look good: take a turn teaching Sunday School, serve as a greeter, help with parking, and so forth. While each of these ministries is necessary and sincerely valued, all of them all internally focused. They all exist to make church life easier, to make our ministries run more smoothly.

We need to remember that "serving" might mean something different from taking a turn in the nursery and teaching a Sunday-school class. While we love and appreciate the hardworking people who serve within our churches, they should do so because that is the calling God has given them, not because they have been pressured into doing it. How many Sunday-school volunteers in your church find such joy in their ministry that you could never convince them not to work with the kids? These are the ones who have found their true ministry and are reaping the fruit of the Spirit.

You have a responsibility to those in your congregation, and if you equip your people but never release them, you have done only half the job. Empowering the congregation means that you must step away. You must teach your congregants that their roles in building the kingdom of God are important—as important as any one of the fivefold ministry gifts—and then you must release them to do what God has called them to do. The atmosphere in your church needs to be one that expects people to go outside the four walls of the church to minister to others, not just to be ministered to as the "audience" of your Sunday-morning "show."

READY FOR DUTY

Part of the work of the Holy Spirit is to place within His children the desire to fulfill the Great Commission. Nothing else satisfies—not good preaching, not good programs for their kids, and not getting out in time to beat the lunch rush. In a church that is fully alive, the people will yearn to do what Jesus did: spread the gospel, heal the sick, and cast out demons. The worst thing a pastor can do is try to stop them.

Have you made it clear to your congregants that they, individually, have this ability? Is it expected of them, or is it considered to be extra credit as long as they show up on Sunday? The people in our churches will have a hard time flowing in their gifts if we pastors don't allow or encourage it. They will have a difficult time praying for healing for someone if they have not first been prayed over themselves. They will be unsure of how to cast out demons if they don't have a clear understanding of the authority that Jesus Christ has given them and the expectations He has for them.

Sadly, most Christians today don't think of their walk with Christ in terms of a battle. If the members of a congregation can recite the verses about putting on the armor of God but have no clue how to cast out a devil, their pastor has failed them. Their pastor has led them to believe that if these gifts are available today, they are reserved for only a select few. Or, worse, their pastor has failed to tell them that the devil is actively seeking to destroy individual Christians in this day and age. They have been taught that the Great Commission of Jesus' church—to spread the gospel, heal the sick, and cast out demons—does not apply to them. Rather, they believe that their primary role, as children of God, is to serve their pastor by helping to make the church run more smoothly.

Pastors underestimate their congregations if they don't expect them to be able to accept the charge to expand God's kingdom. People are desperate to put their faith to work, and they look to their pastors for teaching on how to do it. In their spirits, God has revealed to them that they have been made for great things. When they are told, "Yes, you are! Now, go do your great thing in the nursery," the kingdom of God is sold short.

If pastors allow the Holy Spirit to be in charge, not only will the church always have enough people to work with the kids, but the ones who are in the nursery and Sunday-school classrooms will be those who are called to that ministry, and they will be using their gifts to pray over the children and to raise them up as mighty warriors! We will be astounded by the young men and women our children grow to become when people with the right gifts and callings are put in charge. I will tell you this: The middle schoolers should be doing a whole lot more than studying Jonah and the whale. They should be actively laying hands on one another, praying for one another with power, and exploring the gifts of prophecy and evangelism that their Father may have placed within them. If they don't do these things within the safety of the church, where will they feel comfortable enough to do so?

People young and old know that they are called to reach others with the gospel, yet many pastors do not allow them to fulfill the roles for which their heavenly Father created them. For instance, if pastors choose as mission targets only those ministries that are located halfway around the world, thereby bypassing the poor and hurting right in their own neighborhoods, they are effectively telling their congregations that the only way they can minister is with their money. Many Christians today have accepted the argument that some are called to go, while others are called merely to provide financial support.

But here's a question: Why should the missionaries overseas get to have all the fun? Why should they be the only ones who get to witness the blind seeing and the deaf hearing and the lame walking? Why should they be the only ones who get to do even greater things than Jesus did? Why shouldn't these things be taking place right in our own neighborhoods? Are there no hurting people where you live?

The battle to advance the kingdom of God is the hands of every believer, not just those in fivefold ministry positions or those serving overseas. The Holy Spirit wants to move with power through every person in every congregation. He wants all believers to rise up from the pews and go boldly through their week spreading the gospel, casting out devils, feeding the hungry, and healing the sick.

If this is not happening, then their pastors are failing them. It is time that the body of Christ be equipped for the work of ministry and be released into a dying world right outside the doors of the church.

The body of Christ is composed of kingdom builders, and only building the kingdom will satisfy.

8

FOCUS

Human beings are made for action.

We are made in God's image, and He is a God of action. He is love (see 1 John 4:8, 16), and love is primarily an action verb. Love is not a feeling or an emotion or some mysterious thing that we fall in and out of. It is first and foremost an action, and since we were made and called by God to love others as He has loved us, a definite action is required on our part. Jesus said in John 13:34, *"A new commandment I give to you, that you love one another; as I have loved you, that you also love one another."*

When we are saved into a love affair with Jesus Christ, our spirit knows that we are kingdom builders. And when God begins to reveal the actions He wants us to take to build His kingdom, it is an amazing, exciting thing. His plan naturally takes priority in our lives, because He is our top priority. Nothing motivates us to rearrange our lives like hearing a call from the Almighty, saying, "Go here. Do this."

WAITING ON GOD

Since we are made for action, the first thing we want to do is jump right in and get it done! However, it is important to remember that God's calling on our lives belongs to Him, and we must answer it according to His timetable. We are not responsible for making sure it happens, or even for its making sense. God's thoughts are much higher than our thoughts (see Isaiah 55:9), and, thankfully, we are not required to figure them out.

The only thing we are responsible for doing is cultivating our relationship with God. That relationship is what fills us, satisfies us, and sustains us. If we make ourselves responsible for the details of the journey, for working out every step along the way, we will either get a big head because things are happening "according to plan," or we'll become burned out and discouraged because they aren't.

The Bible says that God talked with Abram (later called Abraham) as a man talks to a man, face-to-face. (See, for example, Genesis 17:1–4.) In the course of this incredible relationship, Abram received quite a calling from his heavenly Father. God gave Abram some very clear instructions—an action plan, if you will. He was to leave his country, leave his father's house, and go into a land that God would show him. (See Genesis 12:1.)

In addition, there was this promise:

I will make you a great nation; I will bless you and make your name great; and you shall be a blessing. I will bless those who bless you, and I will curse him who curses you; and in you all the families of the earth shall be blessed.

(Genesis 12:2–3)

So, there was God's part, and there was Abram's part. Abram was responsible to take the first step: leave his father's house. Other than that, he was expected only to continue his relationship with God, face-to-face, as with a man. In doing so, he would allow God to handle the *when*, the *where*, and the *how* of the whole blessing business coming together.

FOLLOW GOD WHEREVER HE LEADS

Abram was not responsible for becoming great and blessing everyone on earth. God said that He would handle those things. Abram was not given a road map, a complete action plan spelled out for him. He had no need for a map—he had a relationship! And through this relationship, it was revealed that the first step was for him to leave his father's house.

The very next verse says, "*So Abram departed as the LORD had spoken to him*" (Genesis 12:4).

He immediately took steps to move when God said "Move." He didn't know God's part, and he didn't ask. He probably wouldn't have believed it even if God had told him. Abram understood God's directions for the moment, and that was simply to "go."

Now, do you think when Abram got to the end of the block, he asked, "God, should I keep going?" Do you think that after he took a step, he said, "Okay, Lord, I'm not going to move another step until I get a word from You"?

No; because he was in a face-to-face relationship with God, Abram knew God's will for him. He knew that God had told him to go, and he trusted that when God wanted him to stop, He would tell him. When God wanted him to turn left or right, He would tell him. Because of the dynamic relationship Abram enjoyed with his loving Father, he could trust his own steps.

He didn't have to ask which side of the mountain he should go around or when to make camp or when to break camp or whether he should start with his left foot or his right. He simply needed to listen to God.

CATCH GOD'S VISION

When we are driving in a car and taking directions from a passenger, we don't need to ask if we should go straight or turn at every intersection, or whether we should stop at every house we pass. We simply follow the latest instruction, trusting that our guide will tell us when to turn and where to stop.

It sounds simple, but consider how this principle applies in our own ministries: If we have five loaves of bread, and five hungry men ask for a loaf, do we need to pray over each man and each loaf, seeking direction from the Lord as to whether or not we should give him the bread?

Absolutely not! Jesus has already given us direction: "Feed the hungry." (See, for example, Luke 3:11.) That is His will, His vision for what Christians should be doing, and He has not rescinded that command. We don't need to ask for confirmation every time we set out to do something that He has already told us we should do. We need only understand His heart, His vision. That way, we won't worry about silly things like giving away our last loaf of bread. Rather, we will experience the reality that operating in His vision brings us His provision, and we will see that when we move in the will of God, we operate under an open heaven. Natural rules no longer apply.

So, Abram left his father's house. The first place he went was Shechem, where the Lord told him that this land would be given to his offspring. (See Genesis 12:6–7.) Abram thought, *That's awesome—this is my kids' land, part of that "great nation" that I'm going to become.*

In no way did he think that this was the complete fulfillment of what God had for him, because his conversation with God was not a onetime thing. God didn't send His marching orders to Abram and then leave it for him to figure them out. By remaining in constant relationship—eye-to-eye, face-to-face—with the Lord, Abram understood that not only did God tell him to "go," but He also promised to show him where. So, he built an altar to honor the Lord, and then he continued his journey. (See Genesis 12:8–9.)

Along the way, hardships happened. A famine forced Abram to head for cover in Egypt. There, he got himself into a situation where he felt he had to lie to Pharaoh, claiming that his wife was actually his sister. Nevertheless, Abram prospered financially—he was blessed. (See Genesis 12:11–16.) The vision God had given him was coming to pass, even though it wasn't anything like what Abram would have imagined. Yes, he was prospering financially, but he was also hiding out in a foreign country and telling falsehoods about his wife. In any case, Abram understood that it wasn't up to him to make the blessing happen; he was to remain focused on his part—the relationship with his heavenly Father.

He also remembered that the vision was much grander than mere financial prosperity. It involved not only being blessed but also becoming a great nation and being a blessing to all nations. This made it easy for Abram not to be satisfied with the financial prosperity he enjoyed in Egypt. So, once again, not wanting to realize only part of what God had for him, Abram moved on.

Soon, he came to a situation in which he and his nephew parted ways. Abram offered his nephew Lot first choice of which way he would go. Lot looked at his options and chose the eastern lands, which appeared to him to be the better decision. (See Genesis 13:11.) Abram, however, was secure enough in the promise he had received that he didn't worry whether Lot might have been stealing his blessing. He trusted God because of the intimacy of their relationship.

After his nephew Lot moved on, the Lord appeared again to Abram and told him to look across the land, in all four directions—north, south, east, and west—as far as the eye could see. (See Genesis 13:14–15.) Then God said, *"I will make your descendants as the dust of the earth; so that if a man could number the dust of the earth, then your descendants also could be numbered"* (Genesis 13:16).

This rehashing of the vision is very significant. God's timetable rarely lines up with our own, but He understands that it is important for us to be recharged occasionally, to go back and stoke the fire that burned in us when He first revealed it. At times, we need for Him to take us back to that point when it seemed like absolutely nothing could stand in the way of God's vision coming to pass in our lives by sundown tomorrow.

But sometimes we find ourselves in a spot where it seems like that was so long ago, and we just feel worn out. We get so sick of contending for the vision that we don't even want to hear about it anymore. It's during these times that we need to ask God to repeat it to us, one more time, giving us a fresh look and bringing life to the vision He gave us for our ministry way back when, and thereby giving us the courage to talk about it and to dream about it again.

We need to cry out to God, saying, "Father, renew Your vision in my heart! Make my passion burn within me once again!" Because the only thing worth dreaming about is what God says He is going to do. Nothing else will satisfy. If we find ourselves dreaming about a greater glory or personal accomplishments or our next vacation, we doom ourselves to disappointment and failure.

DON'T TAKE MATTERS INTO YOUR OWN HANDS

Years passed by, during which time Abram continued to move about. He continued to be faced with difficult battles, as well as great victories, and he no doubt wondered exactly how and when the complete fulfillment of the vision was going to happen. Because, even though God had reassured him, and even though he had continued to honor the Lord God Most High, the fact was that he still did not have even one son, let alone a huge crowd of descendants. The fullness of God's vision for him—the realization of God's plan for his life—could not take place without a son. The whole "becoming a great nation" business had to start somewhere.

And as Abram's focus gradually shifted away from his relationship with God to the unknown timetable of the fulfillment of the vision, fear began to set in. With the passage of time and circumstances, Abram became fearful. He saw the state of his life—his "ministry"—and, like many of us with our own ministries, he knew in his gut that things were far from where they should be, far from where God promised they would be.

DON'T DOUBT

During times of apprehension, it is critical that we refocus on our love affair with our Lord Jesus Christ. If we obsess on the possible reasons why the vision is not coming to fruition, fear will begin to speak to us, telling us that maybe we heard wrong when the Lord spoke to us. We'll think that maybe God is mad at us. Maybe we dreamed it all up ourselves. Or maybe something we have done, some misstep we made, is canceling our blessing.

Fear will tell you that you don't have enough faith, or that some inner fault over which you have no control is keeping your ministry barren. Fear will try to convince you, when your vision has been fulfilled only partially, that your season has passed, or that the promise you heard was for yesterday, not for tomorrow. Like the serpent in the garden, fear will ask you, "Did God really say…?" (See Genesis 3:1.)

Our heavenly Father understands that our timetable is not His timetable. If we cry out, He will take opportunities to rehearse the vision with us, to reassure us that He has not forgotten us. He will remind us to focus on Him, not on the timetable.

Abram was afraid, and he cried out. The Bible tells us that the Lord came to him in a vision and said, *"Do not be afraid, Abram. I am your shield, your exceedingly great reward"* (Genesis 15:1).

Then, Abram got real with God. He dropped all the canned pious, religious phrases and laid out his heart. "Lord," he said, "how is this going to happen? I know exactly what You promised, but things just don't seem to be working out. I mean, if I'm going to be a great nation, by this time I should at least be a small city, right? And I don't even have a son! What's up? Am I missing it?" (See Genesis 15:2–3.)

I want you to notice something: Abram's response had absolutely nothing to do with God's statement. God essentially told Abram that He, God, was the reward, yet all Abram could talk about was the blessing: How was it going to happen? When was it all going to work out? How would it ever come to pass?

God understood that Abram had lost focus and that he was afraid, because he was looking for the fulfillment of the vision rather than looking at God. This is why God tried to draw him back to what was important by telling Abram that He, God, was his very great reward, not the blessing that he had been promised. Nevertheless, God did take the opportunity, once again, to reassure the worried man that the blessing would indeed come to pass.

He led Abram outside and had him look at the stars in the sky. There was his blessing. God told him that those stars represented the number of his offspring. And as Abram stood there, gazing up at those stars—so many that he couldn't begin to count them—he believed the Lord, and it was credited to him as righteousness. (See Romans 4:16–22.) Abram figured that if God said it, he could believe it, because God had always been faithful in fulfilling His promises to him. The Bible has many things to say about the power of the prayers of a righteous man, and Abram was seen as righteous because he believed fully in God's ability to establish his inheritance.

DON'T MISS THE BLESSER FOR THE BLESSING

But Abraham was still off focus.

Shortly after this episode, Abram jumped the gun. After handling his own part so well for so many years, this man of great faith decided that it was time to assist God with His part. While Abram believed fully and completely in God's promise that he would become a great nation, he was having some serious trouble with the timetable. God's promises weren't coming to pass soon enough for Abram's taste.

He took his eyes off his relationship with God and began to believe that it was his job to jump-start things. He had stopped pursuing the *Blesser* and started pursuing the *blessing* instead. He got the roles messed up—whose job it was to do what—and, with the urging of Sarai, his wife, Abram fathered a child with another woman. Fellas, if you learn one thing from this book, here it is: This is never a good idea.

Abram's decision was completely absent of the Father's desires—it was made purely from the flesh. After years and years of contentedly communing with God and waiting on His direction, Abram changed his focus and assumed a responsibility that was not his. He came into agreement with fear, which told him that things were not happening fast enough.

He got confused as to what the prize was. The prize was not the blessing—the land he would be given, the great nation his offspring would become, the blessing he would be to others. The prize was not the successful fulfillment of his God-given ministry. The prize was the eye-to-eye, face-to-face relationship that he enjoyed with his Lord. As long as Abram remained in pursuit of the Blesser, he would always be blessed, in good and bad circumstances alike. It didn't matter whether he was hiding out in Egypt or roaming free across the desert; he was blessed. As long as he remained in a right relationship with God, he understood the Father's heart and trusted the Father's direction and timing for his ministry. And any questions he had were along the lines of, "God, when will You make this happen?" and "How will You accomplish this?"

But when Abram's focus shifted toward securing the blessing, the nature of his questions also changed. He started asking, "What do *I* need to do to make this happen?" "If *I* do this, will it help my ministry come to fruition?"

And since he was asking the wrong questions, it became nearly impossible to receive the right answers.

Whether or not he should father a child by someone other than his wife was definitely the wrong question! Granted, it was the custom in his society for a wife to offer her maidservant to her husband if she was unable to bear children. But Abram's mistake was in knowing where God wanted to take him and assuming that he knew the best way to get there. He didn't ask God, as he had in the past. Instead, he turned his face from the relationship and relied solely on his own wisdom.

The folly of his decision became apparent almost immediately. In fact, Hagar, the maidservant, was still pregnant when she began to despise Sarai. During this time, I would venture to guess that Abram found very little peace in his household and probably preferred to spend his free time alone on his rooftop. I imagine he looked back at his long travels—all those difficult times in foreign lands, the hard battles fought—and quickly realized that something was different. There had been a shift in heaven.

In the old days, no matter the circumstances, God's fruit had always been evident. There had been peace, love, and joy. The lives of those who follow God's direction will always bear God's fruit. While He may call us to be patient, He does not call us to suffer to prove how much we love Him. He does not call us to turmoil, bitterness, and unhappiness. Rather, when we are where He wants us to be, we will be infused with peace, even in the midst of trials. There will be love, even in disagreement. And there will be joy, even in waiting.

But with Hagar, let's just say it was evident that this was not in line with God's plan. While their union produced a son, Ishmael, it did not yield any fruit in the kingdom, and it took Abram no closer to fulfilling God's vision for his life. Abram was no longer in right relationship with Father God. Instead, he was reaping the harvest of his flesh. Prior to this, whenever Abram had focused on God and asked about the fulfillment of the blessing, God had reassured him. This time, when Abram focused on the blessing and forged ahead on his own, he birthed a counterfeit version of God's true blessing. It met all of the outward requirements, but it was not blessed by God, because it had been birthed by man.

TRUST THE PROMISER MORE THAN THE PROMISE

In our own ministries, it is very easy to become frustrated with God's timetable, especially once He has made His vision clear and real to us. It is tempting to create a counterfeit vision from the flesh and ask God to bless it. Many of us do exactly this when we turn away from the love affair with our heavenly Father. The *promise* becomes more important than the *Promiser*, and we birth an Ishmael, only to find that the counterfeit promise continually battles against the true promise.

If the peace and the joy have gone out of your ministry, if the whole thing wants to make you go sit on the corner of your rooftop, you need to double-check exactly what it is you're struggling to achieve. Are you longing for the face of Jesus, or are you striving for a successful ministry?

The prize is not the promise; the prize is Jesus Christ! He is the "Pearl of great price." (See Matthew 13:45–46.) The reason people become frustrated with God's timetable is because they become fixated on the fulfillment of the vision rather than on the One who fulfills it. You cannot possibly get frustrated with God's timetable if you are staring right into His face. At that point, nothing else matters—He is the prize!

If I take a big picture and hold it right up to my face, right beneath my nose, I can't see anything beyond that picture. If my enemy is standing behind the picture, I can't see him. If there is a great storm going on, how can I possibly be afraid? I'm not even aware of it! If I am face-to-face with Jesus Christ, nothing else matters. I am so in love, I can't even see my enemy. I can't chase other Gods. I can't be afraid.

Is it possible for me to turn away? I can choose to. At that point, I will become frustrated with the details and angry that not everything is going smoothly. The only thing I will see in front of me are the problems, and my joy will begin to slip away because I have taken on all the responsibilities of making God's vision come to pass. I have taken ownership of the infinite number of details that only an infinite God can work out. I have forgotten that He is my reward, and that only in Him do I live and move and have my being. (See Acts 17:28.)

Here is a trustworthy fact: At any time in my life, on any step along the way, I can turn my eyes from God and look at the road ahead, and I will see ten thousand reasons why the vision God has for my ministry is impossible. And that is where we find Abram—he was focusing on making the vision happen, while living with an angry, barren wife who hated the mother of her husband's child, the one who was supposed to be the fulfillment of God's great promise.

It must have been obvious to Abram that this was not right, because if this child was to be a blessing to the whole world, certainly the child would have been born to his own wife in his own tent, right?

In any case, after taking his eyes off God, birthing a counterfeit blessing, and hurtling down the wrong path for fourteen years, Abram was met at the door of his tent by the all-powerful One. And his first thought must have been, *Uh-oh!* But the first thing God told Abram was to walk before Him and be blameless. (See Genesis 17:1.) Isn't that awesome? God shows up and sees your mess. You know it's a mess, but you're not sure why. You've done everything you can to fulfill the calling He placed on your life, but it just isn't happening. Things aren't clicking like you know they're supposed to. You've screwed up, and you know it, and you know that He knows it, too.

But the first thing God says is, *"Walk before Me and be blameless"* (Genesis 17:1). In other words, "I know what you've done, but you need to know how I see you before we go any further. I choose to see you without blame. Now, let's move on."

God changed Abram's name to Abraham, because, He said, *"I have made you a father of many nations"* (Genesis 17:5). He spoke as if it had already been done, even though Isaac wasn't due to be born for another year. In fact, it was already done many decades before, when Abram first believed in the promise and the ability of God to make it happen.

But now, when Abraham and Sarah (Sarai's new name) were at an age and a place in their lives when having a child would certainly qualify as a bona fide, no-doubt, only-God-could-do-this miracle, they had a son. And, for Abraham, there was no doubt that he was finally smack-dab in the middle of God's plan for his life. He sent Hagar and Ishmael away, and concentrated fully on the true plan that God had for him. The joy was back. There was a shift in the atmosphere as Abraham completely released the counterfeit promise and grabbed hold of God's true plan for him.

As Isaac grew, everything finally seemed to be on track. The fullness of the vision was coming into view. This young man chosen by God would soon have a family that would be as numerous as the stars in the sky. He would be blessed, and all families on earth would be blessed through him. Isaac truly was the fulfillment of the promise that God had made to Abraham. He was the future. And it was right at this moment, when everything was so perfectly aligned, that God came to Abraham and said, in effect, "Take the boy up to Mount Moriah and kill him." (See Genesis 22:2.)

Wow.

All of a sudden, Abraham had to answer a question: Was Isaac, who represented the promise, his everything? Or was God his ultimate reward? The old Abram hadn't understood when God had said, "I am your very great reward." It hadn't clicked. Abram had been too focused on the blessing instead of the Blesser. But now, his choice was clear: He had to make the correct choice this time. Did Abraham love his son? Of course! Isaac represented the completion of God's vision. He was the object of Abraham's faith. His son was the gift that he had believed God for. But now, the very same God who had promised and delivered a dream was telling Abraham to discard that dream.

We can only imagine what was going through Abraham's brain as he climbed that mountain. He loved his son; he loved the calling; he loved the future and the promise. But he loved God more. God was his reward. He loved God more than he loved the vision, and so he was willing to put a knife to the throat of the vision, even though it was a promise given by God.

In our own lives, and in our own ministries, we need to get to the point where we can truly say, "Even if I never fulfill the dream, even if I never walk in the vision that God has for me, I'm okay, because just having an eye-to-eye, face-to-face love affair with Jesus is enough."

And watch this: When Abraham made that choice, Isaac lived! God stepped in and spared his life, saying, "*Do not lay your hand on the lad, or do anything to him; for now I know that you fear God, since you have not withheld your son, your only son, from Me*" (Genesis 22:12). When, like Abraham, we get to the place where we choose our relationship with God over our vision from Him, then our vision will finally live, and the provision of God for its fulfillment will finally come. When we get to the point where we are fulfilled—fully satisfied—whether or not we ever walk in the future blessings and prosperity that God has promised us, only then will our priorities be in order, and only then can God fully and completely bless us.

The calling of God on our lives—the vision He provides of the plans He has for our future—is an incredible thing. It is an insight into the mind of God, and a picture of where we will be the most effective for His kingdom. That is not to be taken lightly. A vision from God, a true calling on our lives, is something around which we should order our entire focus.

But the vision cannot be allowed to become the reason for everything. At the very core of what motivates us, there must be an ongoing love affair with the Person of Jesus Christ. We need to find our contentment, our passion, and our purpose in a one-on-one relationship with the King of Kings, because, along the way, the vision will stall—there will be doubts and trials and incredible disappointments—and if they become our only focus, we will quit; or, worse, we'll keep on going without bearing God's fruit. The only thing that will give us the ability to persevere and be fruitful is an ongoing love affair with Jesus Christ.

If our sense of well-being and purpose comes exclusively from the things we do, we are destined to fail, because, frankly, some days, we're firing on all cylinders, and some days the car won't even start. So it can't be about what we do. It has to be about who we are.

If we are a sold-out, on-our-knees lover of Christ, then we are worth something—not because of what we accomplish but because Christ paid a great price for us. If we hold a successful ministry as our prize, we've missed it. *He* is the prize. *He* is our very great reward.

WHEN WE WORK, GOD DOESN'T

It was in the Dominican Republic that I had the great privilege of traveling with Mel Tari. In addition to being the author of *Like a Mighty Wind*, Mel is also a mighty evangelist at the forefront of an incredibly powerful ministry for God. I remember reading his book when I was in school, and it just blew me away. Now, here I was, having the great honor of traveling with him.

On our first stop, we went into a town that didn't look very big at all. I was absolutely amazed to see people pouring out from all around us to see Mel. They were walking miles, coming from all over, to see this man speak.

The meeting was in a huge auditorium jam-packed with thousands of people. Mel gave his message, and as he was preparing to give the altar call, I took my eyes off him for just a second to look at the crowd. When I turned back again, Mel was gone. I looked around, trying to see if he had walked out into the crowd or had ventured offstage, but there was no

Mel to be found. I kept looking at the stage and then at the crowd and then back at the stage from what must have been five minutes.

There was an energy in the crowd, a pressure, and it felt like they were going to start pushing forward at any second. Finally, I rose up on my tiptoes and saw Mel. He was lying down behind the pulpit, not moving.

After fifteen or twenty minutes of this, I was getting nervous. Not that anything was wrong with Mel—I knew that wasn't the case—but I was nervous that the crowd was going to keep pushing forward and overrun the stage. The whole situation was growing increasingly tense.

I looked back at the crowd after what seemed like another ten minutes or so, and in the back, I could see the people parting to make way for something or someone. As they came closer, I could see that it was a man pushing someone in a wheelchair. The two of them were moving forward, forcing the crowd to part as they came.

The gentleman in the chair, I found out later, was about thirty years old and belonged to a local church. He'd had cystic fibrosis since the age of six, and the looks of determination on his face and on the face of his father, who was pushing him, were just incredible. They were going to make it to the stage, whether or not there had been an altar call.

I thought, *Certainly now Mel will get up. He can't let this guy push all the way from the back of this huge crowd and not get up and do his thing.*

But he kept lying there.

It was all so uncomfortable, so awkward. If you've ever been in a place where there's a huge crowd and someone is expected to speak but doesn't, it was that anxious feeling multiplied by ten or twenty thousand. It began to occur to me that perhaps I needed to do something—maybe go over there and pray for this guy in the wheelchair. He'd overcome huge obstacles to make it to this stage, and now he was not even being acknowledged.

Still, Mel wasn't moving.

Suddenly, a few people in the front rows started yelling and screaming. In a few seconds, it grew into a huge roar. The man in the wheelchair was up and walking around. He was smiling and laughing and 100 percent healed!

All that time, I had been waiting to see Mel. I had come expecting a sideshow. I had gotten accustomed to seeing evangelists do certain things in a certain order and then witnessing a certain result, and that's what I was anticipating.

But the man in the wheelchair, along with all the other people, many of whom had traveled miles to see Mel, really didn't want to see Mel—they wanted to see God. And on this particular night, Mel got out of the way, and these people got exactly what they had come to see.

THE LOOK OF A LEADER

Our labor is not to labor.

The spiritual gifts that God imparts to us are not for the purpose of putting on a sideshow. Whether the gifts are operating or not, it's always all about God, never about anything that we do. It's not our job to stand up and work at it, to make the healings and the blessings and the prophecies happen. At best, we are simply conduits through which God's glory may pass, and the more we get out of the way, the more He will be revealed.

Many pastors have developed their "shtick," their routine. Many church services have become exactly that—a routine. If pastors ever overhear people talking about them, saying things like, "Hey, you gotta come see this guy," then they need to check with God to make sure they're not cutting in on His piece of the action. When pastors begin to feel responsible for the end result, they have become involved in the labor. Feeling responsible for the end result automatically assumes that pastors know what the end result should be, and when we do that, in most cases, we limit God. The best a pastor can do is to help prepare the way, for the victory belongs to God.

In the Bible, when performing their service at the temple, the priests were instructed never to wear wool. They were to wear linen only, and sweating was not a good thing. Pastors should keep this in mind, as they work hard to be the best pastors they can be. While they are called to give 100 percent—everything they have—in the end, they can't make ministry happen, no matter how hard they try. The effectiveness of ministry is up to God. He's the Great Shepherd, and we need to place everything in His hands, because He knows best how to meet the needs of His sheep. It is remarkable what God can do on behalf of His children if we will just get out of the way. There is a godly wisdom in removing our muscle and depending on God's miracles, because He cares more about His people than we ever could.

When it comes down to it, your mission is not about you. It's not about the fact that you're the pastor or that you've been called or that you oversee a "flock" of hundreds or even thousands of people. You should never begin to think of yourself as "the Man" (or "the Woman"). The fact is that you have been called to the position of a servant—the lowest position in the church, not the highest—and you must give more than just lip service.

I've got a good friend named Jim. He was our first graduate from Harvest House. He is an absolutely brilliant man, but at some point, his life hit a rough patch, he got hooked on drugs, and he found himself in our program.

Jim is a tall guy with that handsome look of success, and he backed it up by wearing suits everywhere he went. And if you know me, you know that I'm always into working on something, and I'm usually dressed like a bum.

Anyway, Jim and I used to eat at the restaurant across the street from the church, and I began to notice that they always made his salad a little bigger, and his sandwich always had a few extra slices of meat on it. It seemed that they would refill his Coke a little quicker and that he'd get two scoops of ice cream that were way bigger than mine. Then, one day, I went there by myself. After I placed my order, the waitress said, "Hey, where's the pastor?"

"What do you mean?" I asked.

"The pastor—the guy you're normally with."

"I'm the pastor," I told her.

She just looked at me. "No, you're not. That good-looking black guy with the suit—he's the pastor!"

Can you imagine? She was arguing with me, insisting that I wasn't the pastor. She was so convinced, I almost started to believe her.

Many times, the world will look at the nicely dressed man in the pulpit and want to set him apart from the "normal people." We have to be very careful that we don't buy into this and go along for the ride, because in the kingdom of God, it will never have a positive outcome.

If we went back in time and happened upon Jesus and His disciples having a picnic, it probably would be difficult to identify which one was Jesus. If someone asked us, "Which one of these men is the Lord of all creation?" we would likely pick the one whom everyone was making a fuss over. We would pick the guy in the suit—the one with the biggest sandwich.

We would not immediately select the guy who was picking up the dirty dishes and refilling everybody's tea—at least, not until the picnic was over, when He began to wash their feet. Then our knowledge of Bible stories would kick in, and we'd say, "Oh! That's Him! I remember. He told us to do that." It is important for us to remember that Jesus lived His entire life on earth serving others. If He were here in the flesh today, walking among us at a picnic, I don't believe that we could easily pick Him out just based on appearance.

Here's a challenge for you. I call it the "picnic test." At a church picnic, would it be easy for a visitor to identify you as the pastor? Do you stand out as the "leader" of the flock? Are you the one gliding through the crowd, clean and pressed, allowing people to claim a seat for you when you want to sit down? Or are you one of the folks who arrive early to help set up the tables? Do you allow yourself to get a little dirty and—oh, no!—even sweaty from working to get the grill going?

SMELL LIKE THE SHEEP

To be a really effective shepherd, a pastor needs to smell like sheep.

Sometimes, as pastors, we can carry an aura that demands respect. Don't get me wrong; respect for a man's office—any man's office—is certainly due. We don't walk into the meat market and slap the butcher on the back and say, "Yo! I need a pork chop here!" We have to show respect for what a man does. But true respect is freely given, never demanded by the one who receives it. Unfortunately, some of us in the office of pastor have placed a burden on our congregation that stands in the way of true, deep friendship.

Here's another good test: When you walk up to someone in your congregation and ask to have dinner with his family, is he truly excited about the prospect, or does he become nervous and uncomfortable? If he feels the need to rush home and clean the house and scrub the toilets and haul out the fine china, how close of a relationship do you really have with him and his family? Do they do that for their true friends?

Many Bible colleges teach that there are the fivefold ministers—apostles, evangelists, prophets, pastors, and teachers—and then there is everyone else—the laity, the flock. Students are told that there is a necessary separation, a division that exists for the benefit of the church.

Frankly, I believe that the emphasis on the office of pastor and the rest of the fivefold ministry has been too high. This separation between us and our flocks is not healthy, despite what we learned in school. (In fact, quite a bit of what we learned in school is not healthy.) The best way we can help our flock is by smelling like sheep. The most effective way to empower a congregation is to have no separation between the leaders and the laity.

I believe in the office of the pastor, and I believe it is an office that should be respected. But I also believe that many people in this office have done it great harm because of their pride and their ego. They got caught up in the seduction of the pulpit and the accolades of man. Sometimes we need to get off our high horse. We need to take off our $2,000 suit and leave the Mercedes-Benz in the garage. We need to remember that we are called to serve, not to be served.

When we start believing that we are the reason people come to our church—that our wonderful gifts are the big attraction—we should watch out. When we start allowing the people in our church to stroke our ego, and when we start to expect it, we're in big trouble. When we start believing our own press releases, we're done.

OBEDIENT, NOT RESPONSIBLE

As long as we stay eye-to-eye and face-to-face with Jesus Christ, allowing Him to be the one to edify us, then our egos won't be susceptible to being stroked by the world. But if we set ourselves up as the rescuers, Jesus Christ can't get the glory. It doesn't matter if we are trying to be rescuers out of a true love for our fellow man or if we set ourselves up as rescuers out of a sense of duty; we cannot be the rescuer. The Rescuer is Jesus Christ, and it must be our love for Him that motivates us to serve His bride.

While it does feel good to serve God and to help other people, we cannot allow ourselves to get hooked on "feeling good." A healthy ministry should be an overflow of a love affair with Christ. It is important to make the distinction that we do not love Christ by doing ministry; rather, we do ministry because we love Christ. A good analogy is that of tithing: We do not love Jesus by giving money; acceptable tithes and offerings should be the overflow of our love affair with Jesus.

When it comes to feeding the hungry and helping the poor in other ways, we can meet their needs for the sake of the kingdom, or we can meet their needs because it makes us feel good. The latter path is a trap, because it sets us up as rescuers. We become the reason that the people get fed, clothed, and otherwise helped, and we get the glory. But if we are meeting their needs for the sake of the kingdom, God alone will get the glory. At that point, God is seen in His role as the Rescuer, and He is responsible for the futures of the people we are serving—not us.

When it comes to the Harvest House rehabilitation program, many people ask, "Exactly what are the end results? How many of the men and women who come through your program are still serving God?"

The truth is, I don't know. I'm just being obedient. And I always tell them as much.

"Yes, but are you truly helping them?" they ask.

I tell them, "I'm not the rescuer; I'm just a servant."

"Well, when you're handing out all of this free food to people, how many of them are coming to church?"

"It doesn't matter."

"Where are all these shoes gonna end up? Are the recipients going to Christians?"

I don't know. I'm being obedient. If I take it further than that, I become "responsible" for the outcome, and the truth is, it's not my responsibility. Even the farmer plants in faith. God gives the increase. God is responsible for the end result. The food, the clothes, the rehabilitation programs are not about rescuing God's children; they are all about introducing them to the Rescuer, Jesus Christ.

If we become the rescuer—if we make the decision that it's up to us to rescue the people, then we have fallen into the trap. We have allowed ourselves to believe that we really can fix it. In ministry, if we're the fixer, Christ doesn't get the glory.

God is a jealous God (see, for example, Exodus 34:14), and when we allow pride to enter in, we develop a dependency on the feeling that comes from helping the "lesser." The act of doing will become about boosting our sense of worth rather than about acting obediently as a child of God. We will forget, or at least minimize, the fact that we are worth something because we *are* a child of God, and that Christ paid a great price for us.

Unfortunately, many people who have a bent toward ministering to the broken are people who are themselves broken, people who have had a taste of the same type of problems as the people they are trying to rescue. They minister out of their brokenness, using ministry as a means of making themselves *feel* whole. But our wholeness does not come from reaching the broken. Our wholeness comes from our love affair with Jesus Christ.

When we stand in the pulpit with a mind-set of a rescuer, it is the beginning of a rocky road of attempting to do the work of the ministry without the help of the Spirit of God, trusting in our own power instead of in God's power. It is the beginning of people getting hooked on us rather than on Jesus Christ.

I used to pray, "Let my sermons be anointed," or "Let me draw a great multitude," so that I could feel better. I used to want people to say, "Boy, that Minor, he's a preacher!" Now, I pray, "Jesus, get together with Your kids today. Reveal Yourself to Your children; let them come away and say, 'God whispered in my ear today. I could feel His presence. I could feel His arms around me.'"

NEVER GIVE UP

The making of a man or woman is more important than the making of a ministry.

At the very heart of it, Christ places a higher value on us as individuals than He does on the job He has called us to do. This truth flies in the face of the world's thinking, which says, *I'm only as good as what I accomplish. My worth is found in my deeds, not in the simple fact that God loves me.*

It pains me to know that upwards of 60 percent of young people who leave high school or college and go into the ministry never last there for more than a few years. That percentage is way too high, and I believe a major factor is a failure among these young pastors to allow God to complete His work in their hearts. They place too much importance on the early success of their ministry, and when it doesn't produce fruit right away, they grow frustrated and give up. While they are eager to pursue their great hope of following the call of God, they are not equipped or prepared to hang in there if that hope is deferred.

But hope deferred is not necessarily hope denied.

The fact is that sometimes we get the assignment, or the calling, and we're simply not ready to fulfill it. We need to be made ready. Many times, whether we are called to ministry early or late in life, there is a work that still needs to take place within us before we can be as effective as we can be for the kingdom. There is a process that must be completed first. God can and will use us along the way, but in order for us to see the complete realization of His vision for our lives, we need to be made complete as individuals.

An excellent parallel can be found in the making of pottery. The crafting of such a vessel begins with the unearthing of raw clay (you and me). The Potter has to dig us out of the ground in our crudest, roughest form. At this point, we may have no idea that we are going to be useful, much less a thing of beauty. We think, *I'm just fine the way I am. I'm some pretty good clay; I'll make a halfway decent road or maybe a nice brick.* But the Potter has bigger plans. He begins to work with us, patiently picking out all the rocks and debris. Along the way, water is added, giving us the ability to be formed, worked, and molded. It's not a gentle process! The clay is beaten and stretched. It's mushed and mashed to get all the air out, because the Potter knows that the tiniest impurity, even though not visible now, will cause us to fly apart under the stress of what He has planned for us. Finally, when every last bit of junk has been removed by the Potter, at least we know we are not destined to become a brick. God has put His greatness within us—we can sense it. We are ready to be molded, and we beg to be put on the wheel and formed exactly as He wants us. He places us on the wheel and begins to shape us, and it feels great. We are pliable, workable, ready to be remade. The Potter forms us inward at first, to get our balance just right, and then He moves outward and finally upward. In the hands of the Master Potter, we evolve into an instrument of art, an effective and beautiful tool for use in His service.

It never fails that somewhere along the way in this long process, we start to get excited. We think, *Ooh! I've been taken out of the earth!...Oh—look at all the garbage He's picking out. You mean that was in me? Gross! Wow, I can't believe I'm finally on the wheel! Let's go! Let's go!...Oh! I'm right in the Master's hand; this is perfect! Form me! Shape me! Hot dog, I'm really gonna be something! I'm gonna be useful, and even beautiful.*

Then one day, after all the molding and mashing and shaping and loving, we are removed from the wheel. We see ourselves in a whole new way. We have been designed by the Master Potter for a definite purpose. We are beautiful, not because of anything we've done, but because of the work of His hands. We watch in awe as these hands take us and stick us on the shelf.

And there we sit.

During this time, it may seem like the Potter doesn't even look in our direction. This is certainly not what we expected. Now we think, *C'mon, I was made for great things! I've been called out of the ground by the Master and formed by His hand, until I was exactly the way He wanted me...and now here I am, sitting on this stupid shelf? I'm a beautiful vessel! Put me on a table at a great feast somewhere—I'm ready to serve!*

But at this point, we are not ready. In pottery terms, we are "greenware." This is the drying process. We've been crafted with love and precision, but we're not fully useful yet—at least, not for the incredible things that the Potter has for us. The Master knows that if He presses us into service too early, we will fall apart. He has not yet completed the making of the individual.

This is where our motives are tried and our integrity is built. We must be ready for these times and recognize them as temporary seasons, but ones that serve an important purpose. Like a tree during the stillness of winter, we are to use this time to drive our taproot ever deeper. Even though there is no visible fruit in our life, God's plan is for us to reach for the unending Source that will sustain us during the inevitable dry seasons ahead. This depth is critical to the longevity of our ministry. At some point, we will be tested, and we must find ourselves secure in the knowledge that the Lord is our Source and will never fail us.

ON THE SHELF

This holds true for those who, like pots on the shelf, are waiting for their ministry to take off, as well as for those who are already baking in the kiln. Some people are called into service at a very young age, before this time of testing or curing has had a chance to take place. While God can and does use them in mighty ways for His kingdom, they need to understand that somewhere along the way, they will also experience quiet, still seasons in their ministry—times when the Lord is calling them to move into an even deeper understanding of who He is, times when He wants them to continue to trust Him, even though it may appear in the natural as if things are stalled.

The book of 1 Kings takes us through the initial stages of ministry of the prophet Elijah, and he certainly didn't start small. Right out of the gate, the Lord directed him to go to Ahab, the king of Israel. Ahab had done more to provoke the Lord to anger than all of the kings of Israel before him. God instructed Elijah to proclaim to this king—the most evil and most powerful man in the land—that, as sure as the Lord lived, there would be neither dew nor rain in the next few years, except at Elijah's word. (See 1 Kings 17:1.) You've got to admit, for a youngster in the ministry, Elijah was off to a grand start: talking to kings, controlling the weather, holding the welfare of an entire nation hostage to his command. This was heady stuff!

But just as Elijah's ministry started rolling, the Lord told him to hide, to cut himself off from all contact, and to rely only on a brook for his water and the birds for food. (See 1 Kings 17:2–4.) The *"Brook Cherith"* (1 Kings 17:2) to which he was sent—*Kerith*, in Hebrew—literally means "to cut off" (STRONG, H3772).

Even though it's probably not what he expected, I imagine that Elijah's first day by the brook was pretty rewarding. He was hanging out, drinking the cool water, marveling at the ravens as they brought him bread and meat. He may not have understood why he had been moved to an isolated ravine, but he probably felt that he was still in the middle of God's plan. After all, he'd delivered God's message to the king, exactly as God had instructed him to. Now, in the ravine, he had fresh water to keep him alive and birds coming like clockwork to bring his meals. What an amazing God!

But what was he thinking on the thirtieth day? Or the one-hundred-thirtieth day? How long can a man or woman sit on the shelf before he or she begins to wonder if this is truly God's plan? How did Elijah feel when the brook started drying up because there had been no rain in the land, knowing that rain would not come except at his own word? If Elijah was looking to the brook as his source while it slowed to barely more than a trickle, he was going to be tempted to call forth rain to replenish that which was sustaining him.

He might have begun to think this was a sign from God. *Well, God did say it wouldn't rain until I said so, right? So, maybe this is an open door! It fits so well, it must be a "God thing"! This must be God's plan for me to protect my source, which is obviously drying up.*

As a side note, we really need to watch out when we convince ourselves that something is a "God thing." We are not called to walk through every open door we encounter, only the ones that God tells us to walk through, whether or not they are open or closed.

At this point, relying on his own ability to get the brook flowing again would have been the worst thing Elijah could have done. The brook was drying up because of the drought, and the drought was falling on both the just and the unjust. (See, for example, Matthew 5:45.) One of the greatest lessons for us to learn, as people serving the Lord, is that we are not immune to the harsh realities of life. God had a much bigger plan in mind than merely keeping Elijah's brook flowing. He was trying to bring the people to their knees—trying to make an entire nation turn back to Him.

Although God had called Elijah into isolation from the world, He had not left him alone. God's presence was always there, even though no new marching orders were issued. He was using this time to prepare and strengthen Elijah for what was to come, to complete the making of the man. God knew He had big things planned for Elijah. Through him, God would realign the political structure of an entire nation. Through him, God would wipe out 450 false prophets, as well as the false thinking of His people. Through him, God would even raise the dead. But Elijah would never have been able to serve as a completely effective conduit for God's greatest works if he had relied on anything other than the Lord as his source.

The greatest lesson in the ravine is that the brook is not your source, and neither is the raven; God alone is your source. And He is more interested in forming you into a vessel of honor than in seeing you fulfill your calling. The path that takes you from accepting God's assignment in your heart to actually walking in that assignment can be quite a journey. It may start with a bang and then seem to peter out, or it may seem as though it's taking forever to get rolling. Either way, it is a journey meant to purify you, not discourage you. For the visionary, the man or woman with big dreams and visions burning within him or her, these times of isolation and waiting can be painful, but they are part of a refinement process. God will use them to purify your character as sure as the intense heat of the crucible refines silver.

We don't always know why God calls someone to a brook that is about to dry up. Rarely, if ever, are we shown God's plan all the way through to the end. Sometimes God isolates us and makes us sit by the brook so that the voices of the multitude will grow dim. God will use times of stillness and isolation to draw us closer to Him.

We are the priority of His heart. He wants to ensure that we have ears to hear His voice above all others, eyes to see His vision more clearly than any other, and a heart that chases Him first; because out of that, everything else flows— our direction, our timing, and our entire ministry.

Hope deferred is not necessarily hope denied.

Hope deferred is a process of refinement, but many believers allow themselves to become sidetracked by the activity of the world rather than completing the journey. There comes a point in our lives when, in order for us to have longevity, we must accept that there will be seasons of stillness. That's just the way it is. But in order to finish our course, we have to understand that while God may lead us into the crucible of disappointment—hope deferred, where things are not

NEVER GIVE UP

131

happening the way we think they should—this is simply a step toward our realization that He, and He alone, is our Source.

If the only thing we have to carry into tomorrow is a love affair with Him, that will be enough.

SPITTING OUT THE BONES

We recently had a barbeque at church. I've got this big, black iron grill smoker on a trailer. Brother, it gets the job done: ribs, chicken, beef, whatever. With it, I am the holy-rolling, sauce-flyin', meat-flippin' king of the coals.

At this barbecue, I was standing on my "throne," cooking all this chicken. I'm telling you, people coming to the barbeque could smell the chicken as soon as they turned the corner, even with their car windows up. Others drivers were pulling off the road, because that sweet smoke reached out and grabbed them. And of course, to go along with the chicken were all the fixings of a good cookout: beans, potato salad, breads, and pies. But as soon as you walked up, there was no confusion as to why you were there. It was all about the chicken. To this day, when I look back on that cookout, the chicken is what comes first to my mind. It was crispy on the outside, coated with a sticky sweet sauce, and blackened in spots where even the fire couldn't resist giving it a lick. The meat was so full of juice that it was hard to keep it from dribbling down your chin as you ate. It was the perfect summer afternoon.

But out of all those good memories, you know what escapes me? The bones.

I'm sure they were there, but, try as I might, I just can't remember anything specific about the bones. My memory quickly returns to the juicy meat, or the sweet smell of the grill, or the gracious fellowship of the people gathered there.

And that's how it's supposed to be, because I don't want to remember the bones. I don't want to concentrate on the things that are meant to be spit out and forgotten. I want to remember the good things God provided that were meant to be enjoyed, not the things that were of no use, the things that were in the way. In fact, if you and I were to sit down and talk about that cookout, I could tell you a lot of wonderful things, but we would probably *never* get around to talking about the bones.

Anybody who's ever attempted to fulfill his God-given calling understands that it's a journey. It can take years and years of preparation, but there finally comes a season when your vision starts to become a reality and you finally move into the place where you are operating in your calling. Soon your gift is fully alive and flowing—and right at that moment is when you get the bones.

That's when the nuisances come. Sometimes they are betrayals from people you trusted and counted on. Sometimes they are circumstances that result in the loss of good workers you didn't think you could do without. Sometimes they are people who try to discourage you or to convince you to walk in a role that God never intended for your life. Other times, the "bones" come from sweet, well-meaning elderly people who say silly things, or through downright mean-spirited people who accuse you of the most horrific things imaginable.

Just when God is getting ready to do something through you, the devil begins working overtime, using carnality and human nature to attempt to thwart your success. He doesn't necessarily launch a frontal assault. He's not always roaring in your face. Remember, the Bible says that the serpent was the most cunning of all creatures. (See Genesis 3:1.) He will try to get you to question anything and everything.

In the garden, Satan asked Eve, *"Has God indeed said...?"* (Genesis 3:1). He introduced a seed of doubt, and Eve began to entertain it. Now, her response should have been, "Yeah, God said it; now shut your mouth and go away!" But if she had said that, our Bible would be a lot thinner.

If we are not careful, we can start to entertain the questions of others, well-meaning or not: "Are you sure this is God?" "Did God really tell you to do that?" "Is this the best decision for your family?" "What about the finances?" "Do you really feel equipped to do this?" "What training do you have?"

Many times, skepticism results when human nature is out of sync with what God is trying to do. It is very subtle and often innocent, but it can become a huge nuisance. The Bible says that it's *"the little foxes that spoil the vines"* (Song of Solomon 2:15). So what do you do?

You eat the chicken and you spit out the bones. You look past the small idiosyncrasies and nuisances. You don't rehearse them in your mind, and you don't let them become a part of who you are or what you do.

Not too long ago, I had someone say to me, "Pastor, my family is coming to church this weekend, and I want them to be comfortable." He proceeded to run through a list of all the reasons why we had to change all the things we normally did. The music was too loud. The sanctuary was too cold. We never start on time, and we never finish on time.

I listened, nodded, and smiled (I think). When this person was done, I told him that I was really not in charge of how the services went.

"But you're the pastor," he moaned.

"I know," I said—still smiling, I'm pretty sure—"but we do our best to let God do whatever He wants to do, and we try to keep in step with wherever He goes. My job is to cooperate with the Holy Spirit, be in that place of rest, and let God do what He does. I'm not going to get up there and orchestrate anything."

This was not sitting well with my friend. "Well, you're the pastor, aren't you?" he said. "Can't you do anything about the sound? I don't want my family to come in here for forty-five minutes and have to wear earplugs! And my mom is old; she gets chilly."

I'm fairly certain that I wasn't smiling anymore. Not only was I expected to be in complete control of the service, but I was also the sound guy and the AC guy!

My focus can quickly go from hearing and obeying Jesus Christ to all these other distractions. Instead of focusing on my love affair with my living Savior, I concentrate on all these dead bones.

Every barbecue has bones, unless you're cooking hot dogs. (And if hot dogs are your idea of a barbecue, you need to come see me.) Your ministry will have bones, too—guaranteed. Usually, they come from well-meaning people who don't have a clue. That's okay. Just let their hurtful comments roll right off you. Stay focused on the fact that you're in love with your Lord and Savior, and in the end, when you look back, you'll remember only the tasty chicken, not the bones.

TAKING GROUND

It's easy for Christians to look at the underdeveloped nations of the world and identify places where the gospel is fighting to gain a foothold. We can recall times in the recent and distant past when great revivals took place, and recognize the territory that was won for the kingdom of God. What is sometimes not as evident to us is the ground that has been won and subsequently lost within our own congregations. This usually happens when the spiritual temperature of a church is more dependent on the fire of an individual leader than on the fire of God. When this happens, and the current generation moves on, there is little left behind for the next generation to hold on to.

Many U.S. churches are tempted to evangelize Third-World countries because the results—the ground that is taken back from the enemy—can be dramatic and obvious. But if we don't concentrate on taking ground and holding it within our own congregations, we may be issuing a death sentence to our own churches. We may be ensuring that all the victories won in pursuit of the kingdom will die with us.

Every generation fights for something, and, too often, I believe successive generations yield that hard-fought ground too easily. This is evident not only in Third-World countries (where well-meaning Christians often baptize thousands but don't stay to help the people with their daily struggles), but also on the streets of our inner cities and in the pews of our churches. One of the great ploys of the devil is to entice each generation to fight for ground that has already been taken. As Christians, it is imperative that we build upon the successes of previous generations, and the only way to do this is to tap into that timeless power—the Holy Spirit of God.

The fight for ground within the walls of our own churches is obvious if you know what to look for. When congregations stopped using hymnals and started singing modern songs and choruses based on Scripture, some people couldn't handle it. At one time, the notion of a woman preaching was absolutely unheard of. It was almost like committing adultery to let a woman into the pulpit. There are some denominations that still feel that way. Speaking in tongues is another issue. At one time, if you spoke in tongues, you were considered to be crazy or even a heretic. Not so anymore. Today, there are all kinds of denominations that sanction speaking in tongues, even some that used to speak out against it.

Of course, there are probably some who did not make it past the previous paragraph simply because I mentioned tongues. And that's a shame, because that kind of fear is a weapon the devil uses to keep the church fighting civil wars within its own walls. He forces us, or allows us, to wage internal battles over our precious traditions, when we should be taking ground for the kingdom of God. This book was not written to be an endless series of arguments for or against those things that make up the church today. The fact is, I know miracles are for today, just as they were for the church in Jesus' day. I've experienced them. I know that God still heals, because I've seen it happen. It doesn't matter what denomination you subscribe to; when you stand in the middle of a field in Mozambique and lay hands on a blind man in the name of Jesus, and his sight returns, doctrinal arguments sort of fade into the background. They are really not important anymore.

What is important is God's heart for His children. That's all.

It doesn't really matter whether we sing fast or slow, whether we read from the King James Version or from *The Message* Bible, or whether or not our service gets out exactly on time. What is vitally important is that our loving Father, the Creator of the universe, desperately wants to have a relationship with each one of us. He wants to shower us with His love. He wants to deliver us; He wants to heal us; He wants to prosper us. And He wants us to love Him back, because when we do that, the kingdom is advanced.

Unfortunately, when we insist on doing church as usual, we often create a generation of youth who want nothing to do with their parents' church. At best, these young people break away and start their own churches, where they can worship the Holy Spirit as He is leading them. At worst, they will run away from the church the first chance they get, distancing themselves from all of religion's oppressive rules and empty traditions. Some will return to the church when they marry and have children, but they often end up fighting for the exact same ground that their parents and grandparents fought for.

Some never return.

The true cost of doing church without the power of the Holy Spirit is the loss of the next generation. All of us who have been saved were powerfully attracted to God by the Holy Spirit, and when we remove the Spirit from of our services, we also cancel His magnetic attraction. Then, kids come to church only because their parents make them. Basketball programs and prizes for memorized Bible verses are not enough to hold them, however, and as soon as they're old enough, many of them leave, never to return. There is simply no attraction holding them.

We owe our children better.

RELEASING THE NEXT GENERATION

Along with welcoming the power and gifts and direction of the Holy Spirit, along with casting out religion and tradition, and along with liberating and empowering the people who sit in our pews, we must make a concerted effort to turn over the reins of our ministries to the next generation. There must be an effective passing of the torch.

This requires that the current generation honor the youth of today and prepare them to take the helm. The emphasis on the next generation needs to be one of empowerment, of helping them to operate in their calling rather than simply pacifying them and shielding them from the wickedness of the world.

The ground that has been fought for and won will not be held unless the youth of today acknowledge the work of their parents. However, new ground won't be taken unless the parents allow the next generation the freedom to chase those things that God reveals to them. There has to be mutual honor, for that enables the strength, the zeal, and the passion of the younger generation to carry them forward to accomplish more in a year than the older generation accomplished in thirty years. If they are permitted and encouraged to draw on the experiences of the current generation, our spiritual ceiling will be their launching pad.

Children should not be kept from the official workings of "our" church. It should be seen as *their* church, because, one day, it will be. Youth should be encouraged to lead worship services on a regular basis—with *their* music, not ours. They should preach regularly from the pulpit, expressing the message that the Holy Spirit is revealing to them. They should feel as comfortable praying and laying healing hands on their elders as they do ministering to one another. The Holy Spirit is revealing powerful things to the next generation, and they deserve the freedom to express it in their Father's house.

I believe today's youth are the generation that will reap the great harvest. I want you to read that again. It is a powerful statement with incredible implications.

While the harvest is always ready (see Matthew 9:37–38; Luke 10:2), I truly think that the generation being raised up right now carries a special anointing. They will carry this passion for broken and hurting people without counting their own lives as dear. Around the world, we will see more souls come into the kingdom from every nation, every city, every village, and every tongue than ever before. Even people who were considered to be unreachable will be reached by this next generation.

These young harvesters are not materialistic. The very fact that their parents have recently come through an extremely difficult economic time has shown them that chasing after "stuff" is a fruitless pursuit. They're not interested in titles. When you say "Muslim" to most Christians my age, the hair on the back of their necks goes up. When you point out a Muslim to the youth of today, they say, "Hi, there! Let me tell you about Jesus."

This next generation is not all about convenience. They're not about the "ideal" situation or the "best" youth group or the "perfect" youth pastor. They are a group of kids who have been exposed to the heart of God, and you can see that they're on fire.

They are conditioned and poised to reach the next generation and to reach the world. They are not at all religious. They are not bound by old traditions and norms. To see a mixed-race couple does not strike them as strange at all. They are not going to beat someone over the head just because he's homosexual; instead, they look straight to the heart and know that what the world needs is the Holy Spirit, not more religious rules and traditions.

And they love that the Spirit is in them. They are so ready to pour out their lives, like a drink offering. All the things we have held on to, for the most part, do not interest them. They have discovered the true Pearl of great price. They have caught what matters, and they are ready to pour out their lives for Him, knowing that they may not get them back.

And that is exactly what it's going to take to reap the harvest.

NEW WINESKINS

The best thing that we can do is give our knowledge away to the next generation, for they have the strength and the zeal to take the gospel further than we ever imagined. In his first epistle, the apostle John said that he was writing to the old men because they had the wisdom that comes from years of walking with God, but that he was writing to the young men because they had the strength to overcome the evil one. (See 1 John 2:14.)

Sadly, many older Christians, even those in the pulpit, are reluctant to give their knowledge away, even when they no longer have the strength they once had to take the gospel any further. That is a stinging word, but so many young people have been discouraged because they desperately needed a spiritual father, when all they have been given at their parents' churches are teachers.

The Bible says, *"For though you might have ten thousand instructors in Christ, yet you do not have many fathers"* (1 Corinthians 4:15). A teacher is one who imparts knowledge; a father is one who delights in seeing his sons and daughters put that knowledge to use. As fathers, we say, "Here, let me show you how to catch the baseball, how to swing the bat." We love teaching our children, but, by far, the most thrilling thing is to sit in the bleachers and watch them play the game. We don't want to go out there and hit the ball for them; we want to show them what we know and then let them go out there and do it for themselves. And if they strike out, we yell, "What a great swing!" There's no fear of disappointment in their striking out; we just encourage them to try again.

A great indicator of churches that are on fire for God is the presence of young people. What they are doing may not always look just like the things the adults are doing, and for that, the youth are sometimes ridiculed or sidelined. This is unfortunate, because, if we look back at the great revivals of the past, we see that they usually began with a band of youth who were forced to run off in order to do church in fresh new ways. The things God revealed to them looked different from the things their parents were accustomed to.

When ground is being won for the kingdom of God, we must not relinquish it so casually. Every season of the fight is going to look a little or a lot different from the one prior, as God moves closer and closer to fulfilling His vision for the world. The only way we can be confident that we are in the middle of this great battle is to follow the Holy Spirit, not man-made traditions.

The way we have always done things, and the way our parents always did things, and the way our denomination always does things, means absolutely nothing. What matters is where God wants to take His people in the future. We must be willing to put another generation at the helm of the church, even as we remain in the role of rudder for a season. We must pour into them everything that God has poured into us, and then we must release them.

Every generation has its own challenges for which to fight. We've fought ours, and the next generation will fight theirs. True progress in the kingdom of God comes only if each successive generation does not end up fighting for the same ground, over and over again. Our walk with God is a journey, one in which we should be moving down the road rather than continually circling back. We don't want to be trapped by tradition, religion, doctrinal infighting, or any of the other silly things that churches these days seem to waste so much time and money on.

We need to be open and honest about the battles we've fought during our years in the ministry, especially the internal church battles that we would rather not rehash. That way, the next generation can start where we finish and advance the kingdom farther than it has ever gone. They should be able to stand on the hill that we have won and start their journey from there.

They should go farther, be more powerful, and have more victories for the kingdom of God than we ever dreamed about. Let's not make them waste their precious time fighting the same old battles we did. There are new battles to be waged. There is an enemy to fight. There is new ground to be taken. There are new hills to be conquered that God never even showed us.

A LOVE AFFAIR

The longer I preach the gospel, the simpler the message becomes: God is for me and not against me.

In order to really do pastoring right, this is the number one truth that I need to believe and the number one message that I need to relay to my congregation. In order to be effective for the advancement of the kingdom, and in order to reach other people, I must first allow God to reach *me*. To truly love, I must believe that *I* am loved.

Once I filter out all the religious garbage and get right to the heart of it, God is a loving Father who is always for me, without fail. He is never against me, under any circumstance. He will always do and want what is best for me.

He will not strike me with disease.

He does not send hurricanes as punishment for my country's politics.

While it is certainly true that I sin, I am not a sinner in the hands of an angry God. I am the precious, chosen child of a loving Father, and He created me to have a love affair with Him. His greatest desire is for me to have an intimate, eye-to-eye, face-to-face relationship with His Son, Jesus Christ. Out of all the possibilities, out of all the wonderful things I could do for Him, the thing He desires most is that I simply love Him.

It's easy for me to understand that His greatest desire for me is not to be a super-achiever at work or to maintain a perfectly clean house or to win the fantasy football league. Yet it gets a little hazy when I bring my ministry, my work for Him, into the picture. I can start to think that since He has a job for me, and since He is the One who called me to accomplish His will on the earth, what could possibly be more important? If I pour my life, my heart, my time, and everything I have into this calling, then, certainly, I will win the highest favor from my King. Makes sense, right?

Not necessarily.

In fact, men and women in pulpits across the U.S. today have done a horrible wrong to the bride of Christ by not proclaiming that everyone's first and most important calling is to enter into a love affair with the Person of Jesus Christ. Everything flows from that relationship, and no part of my ministry will flourish, whether I am a pastor or a person in the pew, if that relationship is not real and powerful.

Without an eye-to-eye, face-to-face relationship with the living God, everything quickly becomes just another form of work. Commandments and precepts given in the spirit of love soon decay and harden into nothing more than a bunch of contradictory, love-strangling, life-draining rules. My "work for God" can actually become quite a heavy burden.

LOVE IS THE FOUNDATION

I am called to love Him. I need to know it and preach it. This is the very foundation of what it means to be a Christian. I am engaged in a love affair with Jesus Christ. I am His bride. I am His precious, treasured possession.

The way that He is going to give my life meaning is not through all the wonderful things I will do for Him or the supernatural gifts that He will give me in order for me to accomplish them. It is not even through the great number of souls that He will allow me to harvest in His name. My life has meaning simply because He loves me.

He didn't save me because He needed someone to do His work, and I am not some kind of trophy for His heavenly shelf. He purchased me so that there would be no barriers between us, so that His love for me, and my love for Him, could flow unhindered by the impurity of sin. My life has depth and meaning because of my intimate relationship with Him, not because of the success of my ministry.

If this were not the case, then His love for me would be dependent on how well my ministry was going. And I can't walk down that road very far before I bump into a works-based theology. Granted, they might be good works—they might be the very works that He has asked me to do, equipped me to do, and allowed me to do; nevertheless, they are works, and as long as I see my works as the basis of my righteousness, I will always tend to view those who are doing "less" for God as being less righteous than I. Likewise, I will view those who are doing "more" for God as being more righteous than I.

This type of faulty thinking leads me to a two-tiered, us-and-them Christianity. It makes it impossible for me to believe that God loved the apostle Peter exactly the same as He loves the man lying under an overpass, strung out on drugs. It's impossible to know that He loves me when I stand in the pulpit and deliver an incredible, soul-winning message just as much as He loves the broken man whose demons have convinced him to go shoot up an elementary school full of children.

As soon as I begin to believe that God's love depends on how well I perform for Him, the next obvious questions all have to do with my heavenly scorecard: "How am I doing?" "How are you doing?" "Am I ahead of you, or are you ahead of me?"

This fosters the false belief that in order to "move up," I must do more for the kingdom of God. Sadly, many churches and denominations are built upon this premise, whether it is spoken or insinuated. And it is very destructive, because, sooner or later, it all comes back to what I do rather than what God has done. That is the main reason that some churches suck.

BUILDING ON THE CORE BELIEF

The core of the Christian church is that God the Father loves me, individually, with an unbelievable love, and that He sent His Son to redeem me. It's all about Him—all about His heart, all about what He did, and all about His love for me.

But in today's Western church, that doesn't seem to be enough. I have been conditioned by society to believe that somehow, somewhere, it has to be about me. It has to be about my performance. But performance-based Christianity isn't Christianity at all, whether we are talking about one's congregation or one's performance as a pastor.

From the pulpit, it's easy to buy into this self-centered line of thinking without even realizing it. It's easy to give lip service to who God is and to what He has done, but the messages will begin to sound more like "You need to do this" and "This is why you shouldn't do that." Then, what people do or don't do becomes more important than what Jesus has done. And in a church that should be based on unconditional love, it's amazing to see how much condemnation gets dished out.

If I'm looking at myself in terms of my performance, I might actually think that this mind-set is okay, that it fits. Something about it will feel right; because, after all, when I get real with myself, I will admit that I do fall short. I am a sinner. And God is a just God—He hates sin. So, no matter how much He loves me, He can't let my sin go unpunished. Right?

JESUS PAID THE PRICE

The message of the cross is that I am saved by grace through faith, because God supplied His Son Jesus as the perfect sacrifice. As the Bible says, *"For by grace you have been saved through faith, and that not of yourselves; it is the gift of God, not of works, lest anyone should boast"* (Ephesians 2:8–9). Too often, pastors are tempted to start on that rock and then head in the wrong direction. Instead of preaching that God loves His children and how they ought to concentrate on Him, the message might be something like this: "He loves you, and in order to earn that love, you need to concentrate on you. You need to focus on *your* sin, and on *your* past, and on all the areas in which *you* have fallen short. You need to find and fix all the reasons you're not worthy of His full love. Yes, He died for you, but we both know you didn't deserve it, because even though He cleaned and restored you, look what you've gone and done since then! What about this sin you committed yesterday, or the sin you're standing here in the middle of right now? Isn't this the exact same sin you repented of last week and promised God you were done with? Wow, He must be really disappointed in you!"

Sadly, condemnation like that is often left to stand unchallenged. Many Christians walk out of church carrying this unbearable load of guilt because they've been told that they've fallen short and that God is fed up. They begin to feel that they are one sin away from God raining down His fire of wrath on them—or, worse yet, that He's turned His face away from them. He's so disappointed with them, He simply cannot be around them right now.

GOD'S WRATH HAS BEEN DEFERRED

What we need to believe, in the pulpit and pew alike, is that any anger, any wrath, and any vengeance that God held for us has been fully and completely satisfied at the cross of Calvary. That was where He poured out, once and for all, any punishment that we deserved for any sin that we have ever committed, are committing now, or ever will commit in the future. He emptied His condemnation onto His undeserving Son Jesus Christ, who willingly offered Himself as a substitute in our place.

So now, in God's eyes, it is done. Complete. In fact, to say that God is angry with us over a sin we are committing now, or some huge thing we've done in the past, is to tell Him that His Son Jesus was not a perfect or complete enough sacrifice. But the reality is that our sin does not outweigh His Son's death. Jesus' blood covers it all; therefore, there is simply no more anger, no more condemnation, no more punishment for

God to pour out on us, no matter how badly we screw up. As the Bible assures us, *"There is therefore now no condemnation to those who are in Christ Jesus"* (Romans 8:1).

As children of God who have been covered in the blood of Jesus Christ, we are sinless in the eyes of our heavenly Father. Any guilt we put on ourselves now is completely counterproductive in bringing us into the fullness and completeness of life that God has for us. We simply cannot guilt ourselves into a life of victory.

Here's my disclaimer: I am obviously not suggesting that God's gift of grace allows us free rein to sin. That is a discussion for young Christians who are still on spiritual milk. What I am saying is that we can't suffer enough to make things right with God. As much as we may try, we can't beat ourselves up enough.

WE ARE FREE FROM GUILT

As a believer, if you allow yourself to live beneath such a great burden of guilt, your eyes will become focused completely on yourself rather than on Jesus Christ. Instead of being free to love Him, you will begin to see yourself as one who is condemned, and you will spend all of your time consumed with the price you must pay.

You will convince yourself that because you did some awful thing, you don't deserve the best of God today; that because you struggle with sin now, God can't possibly use you as an instrument of His perfect love in the life of someone else. You won't even believe you have the moral authority to pray for others, much less cast out demons from them or give them a word of prophecy. All of your thoughts will be geared toward paying off this terrible thing you've done, and you will operate under the belief that once you make things right with God, once you get this terrible sin under control and become a better person, then you will deserve His blessing. Then you will be useful to Him. Then He can fully love you. That is a terrible fallacy.

GOD'S NOT MAD AT YOU

If I were to preach the above message to you, I would have given you a debt that you could never hope to pay. If, as a believer, you accept that message, it will be a burden that you were never intended to carry. In fact, the only thing that shame and guilt will accomplish is to cause you to keep turning back to the former things, focusing on the very habits that tried to kill you. You will never experience the true victory of realizing that God is not angry with you; that He does not want to condemn you but simply to love you.

If the people in our pews have accepted Jesus Christ as their Savior, they are already free from the debt they owed—they are liberated from the bondage they were in. God will never tell them otherwise, and neither should we as pastors.

The pure message of the gospel, and what we should be preaching, is that you need to know, way down in your "knower," that God really does love you, regardless of how you see yourself. He even loves you right in the middle of the sin you are in, right there in the mess that you have created. Any message that says something different is not from God.

You need to understand and accept that His love is unearned, because when He decided to love you, you were still unlovely. *"God demonstrates His own love toward us, in that while we were still sinners, Christ died for us"* (Romans 5:8). Did you get that? You were still a sinner when Jesus Christ died for you. What that means is that He's not waiting for you to clean up all your ugliness before He'll love you, because it's not about you; it's all about Jesus Christ and what He did. He purchased you with His very life, while you were still filthy. He paid the full price, once and for all time, and He cannot die for you again.

And guess what? You don't need to feel guilty, because He is pleased with His purchase! He is overjoyed with the fact that He chose you. Even with all your faults, He sought you out and personally selected you as His own. He knew what He was getting. God didn't buy you like some used car that He took home, only to start noticing all the things that are wrong with you. He knew your mileage before He paid the price. And even so, God looked at you and said, "This is the one I want. This is the one I love. This is the one I will die for."

For God, it's not about what you do. It's not about the things you do in your flesh, the things you do for the world, or even the things you do in the Spirit for His kingdom. He chose you and purchased you, and He wants the absolute best for you. When He looks on you and looks in you, His every thought is for you. He does not condemn you. You are His bride. He is in love with you as much as He can be, right now, and He's not holding back any part of His love until you straighten up.

The day that pastors get their congregations to stop holding themselves down and beating themselves up (or the day that they stop doing it for them) will be a glorious day. When all of us, pastors and congregants alike, finally look at God and fully accept His love, all our guilt, all our shame, all our fear, and all our condemnation will fall away. That will be the day when we will begin to receive the fullness of the incredible blessings that He has always intended for us.

One of the most damaging fallacies being taught in the church today is that God is angry—angry at the country for taking prayer out of schools, angry at some other denomination for failing to celebrate the Sabbath on the correct day, or angry at us as individuals for continually falling short of perfection. And, the thinking goes, since He is angry, He is rightfully holding back His blessings. God's blessings haven't been held back because He's angry; they just haven't been received by most of His children, and a lot of it has to do with the church's screwed-up teachings! Our shortcomings do not and cannot hold back the blessings of God. He loves us right now as much as He ever has or ever will. He wants the absolute best for us right now. He is for us, and not against us. Right now.

There are so many blessings that God wants to pour out on His church. If we spend all our time focused on the things we shouldn't do or shouldn't have done, we force ourselves to stay in a place where we believe we are not eligible for any of His blessings. Our relationship with God will be more like that of a vassal and his overlord than it will be like a divine love affair.

Yes, He has provided us with a spirit of conviction of sin, to tell us when to straighten up and get right with Him. And when we do—when we repent and give it to Him and ask His forgiveness—it is done.

God, our loving Father, who is always for us and never against us, doesn't want conviction, condemnation, self-flagellation, or guilt. He doesn't want retribution or compensation.

All He wants is to love us.

All He wants is to be in love with us.

All He wants is for us to turn and face Him, eye-to-eye, face-to-face.

The Bible says, *"Behold your God!"* (Isaiah 40:9). *Merriam-Webster's 11th Collegiate Dictionary* defines *behold* as "to perceive through sight…; to gaze upon." To *behold* is to look continuously, more than just a glance, and to make something our focus. We look in no other direction. Peter was able to walk on the water as long as his focus was on Jesus, but as soon as Peter focused on the storm, he began to sink. (See Matthew 14:22–33.) When he remained focused on the One who loved him, the storm had absolutely no effect. Whether Peter sank or stayed afloat had absolutely nothing to do with Peter's sins. It had everything to do with keeping his eyes on Jesus.

This is what God desires, because He knows that when we are focusing completely on His Son, sin will be defeated, and blessings will be received. He doesn't require that all our messes be cleaned up first. He doesn't count our shortcomings against us, and He doesn't keep track of how much faith or how little faith we have. He loves us fully and completely right now, regardless of how much or how little we've done for Him. We are His treasured possession. We are His precious bride.

In some ways, this seems so basic, like Christianity 101, but this is the rock that everything else is built upon. For you, a person in pew at the back of the church, this is all you need to know. When you know this deep down in your soul, church will stop sucking and will begin to fill you with joy and purpose and love to the point that you'll have to run outside and share the good news with others who falsely believe that God is mad at them.

For pastors, this is the key to doing ministry right. As the shepherd of your flock, if you get this right, you can get just about everything else wrong, and you'll still be okay. But if you miss this, if you don't fully believe and passionately teach that God is always for us and never against us, and that

His love for us is not performance-based, then you and your congregation will miss out on the eye-to-eye, face-to-face love affair with Jesus Christ that He has called you to.

And then, eventually, doing church as usual will simply become a burden; and that, quite frankly, would…well, you know.

ABOUT THE AUTHOR

Jim Minor has been preaching and teaching the good news of the kingdom for more than forty years. He is currently the senior pastor of The Harvest Church in Sarasota, Florida, which he planted with his wife, Peggy, in 1984. The church is an integrated congregation that has blessed tens of thousands of people with its outreach. The ministry includes Free Indeed Food Bank and Acts 5th Ave., sources of food and clothing for the needy. Jim also founded Harvest House, a residential, faith-based drug and alcohol treatment center for men, and Esther's Place, a similar center for women. The 130-bed capacity is always filled to overflowing. Another 120 beds in apartments and single-family homes are filled with formerly homeless mothers with children. Recently, local Sarasota authorities asked The Harvest to be one of the lead agencies in providing housing for the homeless population on the west coast of Florida. Jim and Peggy have five children and six grandchildren, all of whom are serving the Lord with them in Sarasota.